the
Plant-Based Cookbook

The Plant-Based Cookbook

13-Digit ISBN: 978-1-64643-275-2
10-Digit ISBN: 1-64643-275-4

This book may be ordered by mail from the publisher. Please include $5.99 for postage and handling. Please support your local bookseller first!

Books published by Cider Mill Press Book Publishers are available at special discounts for bulk purchases in the United States by corporations, institutions, and other organizations. For more information, please contact the publisher.

Cider Mill Press Book Publishers
"Where good books are ready for press"
PO Box 454
12 Spring Street
Kennebunkport, Maine 04046

Visit us online!
cidermillpress.com

Typography: Brother 1816, URW DIN

Image Credits: Pages 15, 32, 36, 40, 50–51, 52, 59, 60, 74, 77, 78, 82, 86, 89, 90, 106, 109, 110, 113, 118, 122, 125, 130, 137, 141, 142, 145, 148, 163, 194–195, 208, 220, 224, 228, 235, 236, and 240 courtesy of Cider Mill Press.

All other images used under official license from Shutterstock.com.

Printed in China

Front endpaper image: Roasted Coffee & Ancho Carrots, see page 103.
Back endpaper image: Kale Chips, see page 37.

1 2 3 4 5 6 7 8 9 0
First Edition

the

Plant-Based
Cookbook

— **OVER 100** —

Delicious, Wholesome
Vegan and **Vegetarian** Recipes

CIDER MILL
PRESS

BOOK
PUBLISHERS

KENNEBUNKPORT, MAINE

Contents

Introduction

Once seen as extreme measures, vegan and vegetarian diets are now championed by health professionals as a step in the right direction. Instead of being met with immediate skepticism, they are now viewed as means of restoring balance to a diet drowning in excess cholesterol, sugar, sodium, and chemical preservatives, excesses that are contributing to troubling health problems in many Western countries.

Seeing people become more invested in their health and celebrate the incredible bounty Mother Nature sets forth are wonderful things, no doubt. But they do tend to overshadow the biggest advantage of the plant-based diet—access to a variety of delicious, wondrous flavors available immediately. One would have to involve themselves in all manner of creative contortions to match the sheer array of enjoyable tastes one would encounter simply by walking through a farmers market and sampling what was on offer. Marry that flavor with the techniques that the contemporary culinary revolution has brought about—many of which you'll encounter in the following pages—and going green is a boon to the palate as well.

Whether it is the comforting character of a soup that you crave, an elegant entree to serve as the centerpiece of a dinner party, a salad that celebrates the freshness of that day's haul from the garden, or a quick snack that doesn't knock you off course, you'll find it within. Chock-full of vegetables and varietals that are often overlooked, these recipes will not only enrich your time in the kitchen, they will make each trip to the grocery store and farmers market feel like it is brimming with exciting possibilities.

For the seasoned plant-based practitioner, we've scoured the globe to make sure there's plenty of new and exciting dishes so they can keep things fresh. For the ardent vegan, there's more than 50 recipes free of animal products, and a number of others that can easily be tweaked to fit that criteria. For the person on the fence about leaving the carnivore life behind, there's no shortage of decadent offerings that will ease the transition. In short, there's plenty for everyone—just the way Mother Nature wanted it.

Appetizers

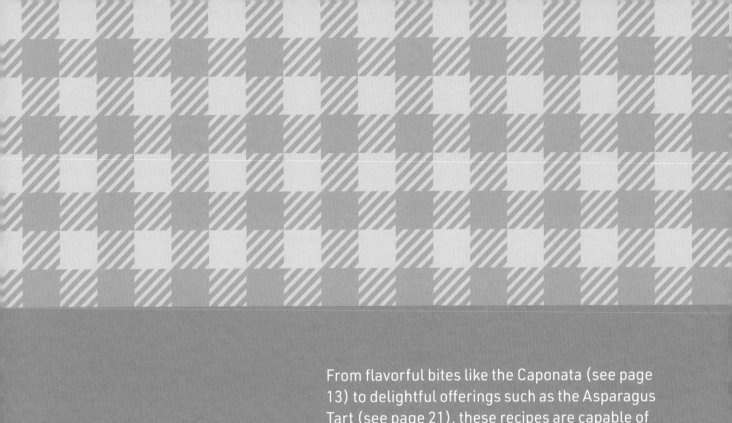

From flavorful bites like the Caponata (see page 13) to delightful offerings such as the Asparagus Tart (see page 21), these recipes are capable of serving as a snack that doesn't lead you astray, as the centerpiece of a platter or serving board, or the launching pad for a memorable dinner party.

Caponata

Yield: 6 Servings

Active Time: 1 Hour

Total Time: 2 Hours

INGREDIENTS

1 large eggplant
(about 1½ lbs.)

2 tablespoons extra-virgin
olive oil

1 onion, chopped

2 celery stalks, peeled and
chopped

3 large garlic cloves,
minced

2 red bell peppers,
stemmed, seeded, and
chopped

Salt and pepper, to taste

1 lb. ripe Roma tomatoes,
peeled, seeded, and finely
chopped; or 1 (14 oz.) can
of crushed tomatoes, with
their liquid

2 tablespoons sugar,
plus a pinch

3 (generous) tablespoons
capers, rinsed and drained

3 tablespoons chopped
green olives

3 tablespoons red wine
vinegar

DIRECTIONS

1. Preheat the oven to 425°F. Place the eggplant on a baking sheet, place it in the oven, and roast until it has collapsed and is starting to char, about 25 minutes. Remove from the oven and let the eggplant cool. When cool enough to handle, roughly chop the eggplant.

2. Place 1 tablespoon of the oil in a large skillet and warm it over medium heat. When the oil starts to shimmer, add the onion and celery and cook, stirring, until the onion starts to soften, about 5 minutes. Stir in the garlic, cook for 1 minute, and then add the peppers. Season with salt and cook, stirring frequently, until the peppers are tender, about 8 minutes.

3. Add the remaining olive oil and the eggplant and cook, stirring occasionally, until the eggplant begins to fall apart and the other vegetables are tender. Stir in the tomatoes and the pinch of sugar, season the mixture with salt, and cook, stirring frequently, until the tomatoes start to collapse and smell fragrant, about 7 minutes.

4. Stir in the capers, olives, remaining sugar, and vinegar. Reduce the heat to medium-low and cook, stirring often, until the mixture is quite thick, sweet, and fragrant, 20 to 30 minutes. Taste, season with salt and pepper, and remove the pan from heat. Let the caponata cool to room temperature before serving. If time allows, chill in the refrigerator overnight and let it return to room temperature before serving.

Nori Crackers

Yield: 30 Crackers

Active Time: 30 Minutes

Total Time: 45 Minutes

INGREDIENTS

1 egg

1 tablespoon water

3 spring roll wrappers

3 sheets of nori

6 tablespoons sesame seeds

4 cups canola oil

Salt, to taste

DIRECTIONS

1. Combine the egg and water in a bowl and brush the spring roll wrappers with the egg wash. Place a sheet of nori on top of each wrapper and brush the nori with the egg wash. Sprinkle the sesame seeds on top and let rest for 10 minutes.

2. Place the oil in a Dutch oven and warm it to 300°F over medium heat. Cut each sheet into nine squares, place them in the oil, and fry until browned and crispy, about 5 minutes. Transfer to a paper towel–lined plate, season with salt, and serve.

Roasted Grapes

Yield: 8 Servings

Active Time: 10 Minutes

Total Time: 1 Hour and 30 Minutes

INGREDIENTS

1½ to 2 lbs. red seedless grapes, rinsed and patted dry

Extra-virgin olive oil, as needed

Salt, to taste

DIRECTIONS

1. Preheat the oven to 350°F. Place the grapes in a mixing bowl, drizzle olive oil generously over them, and toss to coat.

2. Place the grapes on a baking sheet, season with salt, and place in the oven. Roast until most of the grapes have collapsed and are slightly charred, about 25 minutes.

3. Remove from the oven and let cool completely before serving—the longer you let the grapes sit, the more concentrated and delicious their flavor will become.

Savory Tart Shells

Yield: 2 Tart Shells
Active Time: 30 Minutes
Total Time: 2 Hours

INGREDIENTS

2½ cups all-purpose flour,
plus more as needed

⅓ cup extra-virgin olive oil

½ cup ice water

1 teaspoon fine sea salt

DIRECTIONS

1. Place all of the ingredients in a bowl and work the mixture until it comes together as a dough. Divide the dough into two pieces, flatten them into disks, wrap them in plastic, and refrigerator for 1 hour.

2. Preheat the oven to 400°F. Grease and flour two 9-inch pie plates. Place the pieces of dough on a flour-dusted work surface and roll them out into ¼-inch-thick rounds. Lay the crusts in the pan, trim any excess away, and prick the bottom of the crusts with a fork or a knife. Cover the crusts with aluminum foil, fill the foil with uncooked rice, dried beans, or pie weights, and place in the oven. Bake until firm and golden brown, about 20 minutes.

3. Remove from the oven, remove the foil and beans, and fill as desired.

   NOTE: If not using right away, store in the refrigerator for up to 1 week or in the freezer for up to 6 months.

Asparagus Tart

Yield: 8 Servings
Active Time: 15 Minutes
Total Time: 45 Minutes

INGREDIENTS

½ teaspoon kosher salt,
plus more to taste

1 lb. asparagus, trimmed

1½ cups ricotta cheese

¼ cup extra-virgin olive oil

2 tablespoons heavy cream

2 egg yolks

1 teaspoon chopped fresh
rosemary

1 Savory Tart Shell
(see page 18)

DIRECTIONS

1. Preheat the oven to 350°F. Bring a pot of water to a boil. Add salt until the water tastes just shy of seawater, add the asparagus, and cook for 2 minutes. Drain, pat dry, and set aside.

2. Place all of the remaining ingredients, aside from the tart shell, in a mixing bowl and stir to combine. Distribute the mixture evenly in the tart shell, arrange the asparagus in the custard, and place the tart in the oven. Bake until the custard is set and golden brown, about 25 minutes. Remove from the oven and serve warm or at room temperature.

NOTE: This simple custard and the recipe for the Savory Tart Shell on page 18 come courtesy of the simply magnificent Tamar Adler. The pair is so reliable and versatile that any vegetable can comfortably be swapped in for the asparagus.

Fried Squash Blossoms

Yield: 4 Servings
Active time: 20 Minutes
Total time: 50 Minutes

INGREDIENTS

10 squash blossoms,
stamens removed

1 bunch of fresh spearmint

2 cups shredded
queso fresco

Zest and juice of 1 lemon

Salt, to taste

1 cup all-purpose flour

1 teaspoon baking powder

2 egg yolks

1 cup seltzer water

2 cups canola oil

2 tablespoons honey
(optional)

DIRECTIONS

1. Place the squash blossoms on a paper towel–lined baking sheet.

2. Finely chop the spearmint and combine it with the queso fresco. Add the lemon zest and juice, season the mixture with salt, and stir to combine.

3. Stuff the squash blossoms with the mixture, taking care not to tear the flowers.

4. In a small bowl, combine the flour, baking powder, egg yolks, and seltzer water and work the mixture with a whisk until it is a smooth batter. Let the batter rest for 20 minutes.

5. Place the canola oil in a deep skillet and warm to 350°F over medium heat.

6. Fold the tips of the squash blossoms closed and dip them into the batter. Gently slip them into the oil and fry until crispy and golden brown all over, about 2 minutes, making sure you only turn the squash blossoms once.

7. Drain the fried squash blossoms on the baking sheet. Season them lightly with salt and, if desired, drizzle honey over them before serving.

Falafel

INGREDIENTS

1 (14 oz.) can of chickpeas, drained and rinsed

½ red onion, chopped

1 cup fresh parsley, chopped

1 cup fresh cilantro, chopped

3 bunches of scallions, trimmed and chopped

1 jalapeño chile pepper, stemmed, seeded, and chopped

3 garlic cloves

1 teaspoon cumin

1 teaspoon kosher salt, plus more to taste

½ teaspoon cardamom

¼ teaspoon black pepper

2 tablespoons chickpea flour

½ teaspoon baking soda

4 cups canola oil

DIRECTIONS

1. Line a baking sheet with parchment paper. Place all of the ingredients, except for the canola oil, in a food processor and blitz until smooth. Scoop ¼-cup portions of the puree onto the baking sheet and place it in the refrigerator for 1 hour.

2. Add the canola oil to a Dutch oven and warm it to 350°F over medium heat. Working in batches, add the falafel to the oil and fry, turning occasionally, until they are golden brown, about 6 minutes. Transfer the cooked falafel to a paper towel–lined plate to drain and serve once all of the falafel have been cooked.

Chia Seed Crackers

Yield: 30 Crackers

Active Time: 20 Minutes

Total Time: 2 Hours

INGREDIENTS

9 tablespoons chia seeds

5 tablespoons water

½ cup almond flour

½ teaspoon kosher salt

¼ teaspoon black pepper

DIRECTIONS

1. Use a spice grinder or a mortar and pestle to grind 1 tablespoon of the chia seeds into a powder. Transfer the powder to a bowl and add 3 tablespoons of the water. Gently stir to combine and let the mixture rest for 10 minutes.

2. Add the remaining chia seeds and water along with the almond flour, salt, and pepper. Fold until the mixture comes together as a dough, place it between two sheets of parchment paper, and roll out until it is approximately ¼ inch thick. Chill the dough in the refrigerator for 30 minutes.

3. Preheat the oven to 350°F and line two baking sheets with parchment paper. Cut the dough into the desired shape for the crackers and place them on the baking sheets. Place them in the oven and bake until the crackers are golden brown, about 20 minutes. Remove from the oven and let the crackers cool completely.

Tabbouleh

INGREDIENTS

½ cup bulgur wheat

1½ cups boiling water

½ teaspoon kosher salt, plus more to taste

½ cup fresh lemon juice

2 cups fresh parsley, chopped

2 cucumbers, peeled, seeded, and diced

2 tomatoes, seeded and diced

6 scallions, trimmed and sliced

1 cup fresh mint leaves, chopped

2 tablespoons extra-virgin olive oil

Black pepper, to taste

½ cup crumbled feta cheese

DIRECTIONS

1. Place the bulgur in a heatproof bowl and add the boiling water, salt, and half of the lemon juice. Cover and let sit for about 20 minutes, until the bulgur has absorbed all of the liquid and is tender. Drain any excess liquid if necessary. Let the bulgur cool completely.

2. When the bulgur has cooled, add the parsley, cucumber, tomato, scallions, mint, olive oil, black pepper, and remaining lemon juice. Top with the feta and serve.

Eggplant Rings

Yield: 4 Servings

Active Time: 40 Minutes

Total Time: 1 Hour

INGREDIENTS

1 large eggplant, trimmed and sliced

2 eggs, beaten

1 cup all-purpose flour

1 cup panko

1 tablespoon kosher salt

1 tablespoon black pepper

Canola oil, as needed

¼ cup red zhug

¼ cup ketchup

DIRECTIONS

1. Cut the centers out of the slices of eggplant, creating rings that have an about an inch of eggplant inside.

2. Place the eggs, flour, and panko in separate bowls. Add the salt and pepper to the bowl of panko and stir to combine. Dip an eggplant ring into the flour, then the egg, followed by the panko, until the ring is entirely coated. Place the coated rings on a baking sheet.

3. Add canola oil to a cast-iron skillet until it is about 1 inch deep and warm to 375°F over medium-high heat. Working in batches of 4 or 5 rings at a time, gently lay them in the oil and cook until browned and crispy all over, about 4 minutes, turning as necessary. Place the cooked rings on a paper towel–lined plate to drain.

4. Place the zhug and ketchup in a small bowl, stir to combine, and serve alongside the eggplant rings.

Yield: 6 Servings

Active Time: 45 Minutes

Total Time: 1 Hour and 15 Minutes

Tiropitakia

INGREDIENTS

½ lb. feta cheese

1 cup grated kefalotyri cheese

¼ cup finely chopped fresh parsley

2 eggs, beaten

Black pepper, to taste

1 (1 lb.) package of frozen phyllo dough, thawed

1 cup unsalted butter, melted

DIRECTIONS

1. Place the feta in a mixing bowl and break it up with a fork. Add the kefalotyri, parsley, eggs, and pepper and stir to combine. Set the mixture aside.

2. Place 1 sheet of the phyllo dough on a large sheet of parchment paper. Gently brush the sheet with some of the melted butter, place another sheet on top, and brush this with more of the butter. Cut the phyllo dough into 2-inch-wide strips, place 1 teaspoon of the filling at the end of the strip closest to you, and fold one corner over to make a triangle. Fold the strip up until the filling is completely covered. Repeat with the remaining sheets of phyllo dough and filling.

3. Preheat the oven to 350°F and oil a baking sheet with some of the melted butter. Place the pastries on the baking sheet and bake in the oven until golden brown, about 15 minutes. Remove and let cool briefly before serving.

Scallion Pancakes

INGREDIENTS

1½ cups all-purpose flour, plus more as needed

¾ cup boiling water

7 tablespoons canola oil

1 tablespoon toasted sesame oil

1 teaspoon kosher salt

4 scallions, trimmed and sliced thin

DIRECTIONS

1. Place the flour and the water in a mixing bowl and work the mixture until it holds together as a rough dough. Transfer the dough to a flour-dusted work surface and knead it until it is a tacky, nearly smooth ball. Cover the dough with plastic wrap and let it rest for 30 minutes.

2. Place 1 tablespoon of the canola oil, the sesame oil, and 1 tablespoon of flour in a small bowl and stir to combine. Set the mixture aside.

3. Divide the dough in half, cover one piece with plastic wrap, and set it aside. Place the other piece on a flour-dusted work surface and roll it into a 12-inch round. Drizzle approximately 1 tablespoon of the oil-and-flour mixture over the round and use a pastry brush to spread the mixture evenly. Sprinkle half of the salt and scallions over the round and roll it into a cylinder. Coil the cylinder into a spiral and flatten it with your palm. Cover with plastic wrap and repeat with the other piece of dough.

4. Warm a cast-iron skillet over low heat until it is warm. Roll one piece of dough into a 9-inch round and make a slit, approximately ½ inch deep, in the center of the round. Cover with plastic wrap and repeat with the other piece of dough.

5. Coat the bottom of the skillet with some of the remaining oil and raise the heat to medium-low. When the oil is warm, place 1 pancake in the pan, cover it, and cook until the pancake is golden brown, about 1 minute. Drizzle oil over the pancake, use a pastry brush to spread it evenly, and carefully flip the pancake over. Cover the pan and cook until browned on that side, about 1 minute. Remove the cover and cook the pancake until it is crisp and a deep golden brown, about 30 seconds. Remove and cook until crispy on that side, another 30 seconds. Remove from the pan, transfer to a wire rack to cool, and cook the other pancake. When both pancakes have been cooked, slice each one into wedges and serve.

Yield: 4 Servings
Active Time: 5 Minutes
Total Time: 15 Minutes

Kale Chips

INGREDIENTS

1 bunch of kale, stems removed

1 teaspoon kosher salt

½ teaspoon black pepper

½ teaspoon paprika

½ teaspoon dried parsley

½ teaspoon dried basil

¼ teaspoon dried thyme

¼ teaspoon dried sage

2 tablespoons extra-virgin olive oil

DIRECTIONS

1. Preheat the oven to 400°F. Tear the kale leaves into smaller pieces and place them in a mixing bowl. Add the remaining ingredients and work the mixture with your hands until the kale pieces are evenly coated.

2. Divide the seasoned kale between two parchment-lined baking sheets so that it sits on each in an even layer. Place in the oven and bake until crispy, 6 to 8 minutes. Remove and let cool before serving.

Sauces, Dips & Condiments

A large part of taking your plant-based culinary ambitions to the next level is learning how to make foundational items like sauces and condiments yourself. This small commitment ensures that what you're using is fresher than what you can get at the store, and gives you complete control over both the quality and components. On top of all that, they also put you ahead of the game when meal prep time rolls around. Considering all of that, we're confident saying that most of your very best dishes will start with something here.

Hummus

INGREDIENTS

1 (14 oz.) can of chickpeas

3 tablespoons extra-virgin olive oil

3 tablespoons tahini

1½ tablespoons fresh lemon juice, plus more to taste

1 garlic clove, chopped

1 teaspoon kosher salt

½ teaspoon black pepper

DIRECTIONS

1. Drain the chickpeas and reserve the liquid. If time allows, remove the skins from each of the chickpeas. This will make your hummus much smoother.

2. Place all of the ingredients in a food processor and blitz until the mixture is very smooth, scraping down the work bowl as needed.

3. Taste and adjust the seasoning. If your hummus is stiffer than you'd like, add 2 to 3 tablespoons of the reserved chickpea liquid and blitz until it is the desired consistency.

Yield: 8 Cups

Active Time: 30 Minutes

Total Time: 2 Hours

Marinara Sauce

INGREDIENTS

4 lbs. tomatoes, peeled, seeded, and chopped

1 yellow onion, sliced

15 garlic cloves, crushed

2 teaspoons finely chopped fresh thyme

2 teaspoons finely chopped fresh oregano

2 tablespoons extra-virgin olive oil

1½ tablespoons kosher salt, plus more to taste

1 teaspoon black pepper, plus more to taste

2 tablespoons finely chopped fresh basil

1 tablespoon finely chopped fresh parsley

DIRECTIONS

1. Place all of the ingredients, except for the basil and parsley, in a large saucepan and cook over medium heat, stirring constantly, until the tomatoes begin to collapse, about 10 minutes.

2. Reduce the heat to low and cook, stirring occasionally, for about 1½ hours, or until the flavor is to your liking.

3. Stir in the basil and parsley and season the sauce to taste. The sauce will be chunky. If you prefer a smoother texture, transfer the sauce to a food processor and blitz before serving with your pasta.

Yield: 1 Cup
Active Time: 10 Minutes
Total Time: 25 Minutes

Basil Pesto

INGREDIENTS

¼ cup pine nuts

1 garlic clove

Salt and pepper, to taste

2 cups firmly packed fresh basil leaves

½ cup extra-virgin olive oil

¼ cup freshly grated Parmesan cheese

1 teaspoon fresh lemon juice

DIRECTIONS

1. Warm a small skillet over low heat for 1 minute. Add the pine nuts and cook, while shaking the pan, until they begin to give off a toasty fragrance, 2 to 3 minutes. Transfer to a plate and let cool completely.

2. Place the garlic, salt, and pine nuts in a food processor or blender and pulse until the mixture is a coarse meal. Add the basil and pulse it is until finely minced. Transfer the mixture to a medium bowl and, while whisking to incorporate, add the oil in a thin stream.

3. Add the cheese and stir until thoroughly incorporated. Stir in the lemon juice, taste, and adjust the seasoning as necessary. The pesto will keep in the refrigerator for up to 2 days.

NOTE: You can also make this pesto using a mortar and pestle, which will give it more texture.

Perfect Pizza Sauce

Yield: 2 Cups
Active Time: 5 Minutes
Total Time: 5 Minutes

INGREDIENTS

1 lb. peeled, whole San Marzano tomatoes, with their liquid, crushed by hand

1½ tablespoons extra-virgin olive oil

Salt, to taste

Dried oregano, to taste

DIRECTIONS

1. Place the tomatoes and their juices in a bowl, add the olive oil, and stir until it has been thoroughly incorporated.

2. Season the sauce with salt and oregano and stir to incorporate. If using within 2 hours, leave the sauce at room temperature. If storing in the refrigerator, where the sauce will keep for up to 3 days. Return to room temperature before using.

Yield: 4 Cups
Active Time: 30 Minutes
Total Time: 1 Hour

Mole Blanco

INGREDIENTS

1 tablespoon pine nuts, lightly toasted

1 tablespoon sunflower seeds, lightly toasted

1 tablespoon sesame seeds, lightly toasted

3½ tablespoons Vegetable Stock (see page 119), plus more as needed

2 tablespoons extra-virgin olive oil

1½ tomatillos, husked and rinsed

1 garlic clove

¼ white onion

1 tablespoon chopped habanero chile pepper

2 tablespoons chopped turnip

1 tablespoon chopped fennel

1 tablespoon peeled and chopped green apple

1 tablespoon bread crumbs

1 tablespoon sultanas (golden raisins)

1 tablespoon minced plantain

3 tablespoons masa harina

⅛ teaspoon white pepper

⅛ teaspoon ground allspice

Pinch of ground fennel seeds

1 coriander seed, toasted and ground

3½ tablespoons milk

1 teaspoon grated white chocolate

DIRECTIONS

1. Use a mortar and pestle or a spice grinder to turn the pine nuts, sunflower seeds, and sesame seeds into a paste, adding stock as needed.

2. Place the olive oil in a Dutch oven and warm over medium heat. Add the tomatillos, garlic, onion, habanero, turnip, fennel, apple, bread crumbs, sultanas, and plantain and cook until the onion is translucent, about 4 minutes, stirring so that the contents of the pan do not take on any color.

3. Add the paste, masa harina, white pepper, allspice, fennel, and coriander and stir to incorporate. Add the milk and stock and simmer until the fruits and vegetables are tender.

4. Stir in the white chocolate. Taste and adjust the seasoning as necessary.

5. Transfer the mixture to a blender and puree until smooth. Strain before using or storing.

Sweet Corn & Pepita Guacamole

Yield: 4 Servings
Active Time: 15 Minutes
Total Time: 30 Minutes

INGREDIENTS

1 ear of yellow corn,
husk left on

1 oz. pumpkin seeds

1 oz. pomegranate seeds

Flesh of 3 avocados

½ red onion, chopped

½ cup fresh cilantro,
chopped

1 teaspoon fresh lime juice

Salt and pepper, to taste

DIRECTIONS

1. Preheat a gas or charcoal grill to medium-high heat (about 450°F). Place the corn on the grill and cook until it is charred all over and the kernels have softened enough that there is considerable give in them.

2. Remove the corn from the grill and let it cool. When cool enough to handle, husk the corn and cut off the kernels.

3. Combine the corn, pumpkin seeds, and pomegranate seeds in a small bowl. Place the avocado in a separate bowl and mash until it is just slightly chunky. Stir in the corn mixture, the onion, cilantro, and lime juice, season the mixture with salt and pepper, and work the mixture until the guacamole is the desired texture.

4. Taste, adjust the seasoning as necessary, and enjoy.

Sweet Corn & Pepita Guacamole, see page 49

Yield: 1½ Cups
Active Time: 20 minutes
Total Time: 30 Minutes

Salsa Verde

INGREDIENTS

1 lb. tomatillos, husked and rinsed

5 garlic cloves, unpeeled

1 small white onion, quartered

10 serrano chile peppers

2 bunches of fresh cilantro, leaves and stems

Salt, to taste

DIRECTIONS

1. Warm a cast-iron skillet over high heat. Place the tomatillos, garlic, onion, and chiles in the pan and cook until charred all over, turning them occasionally.

2. Remove the vegetables from the pan and let them cool slightly.

3. Peel the garlic cloves and remove the stems and seeds from the chiles. Place the charred vegetables in a blender, add the cilantro, and puree until smooth.

4. Season the salsa with salt and enjoy.

Yield: 2 Cups
Active Time: 15 Minutes
Total Time: 45 Minutes

Chipotle Salsa

INGREDIENTS

3½ oz. chipotle morita chile peppers, stems and seeds removed

5 Roma tomatoes, halved

1 small white onion, quartered

5 garlic cloves

Salt, to taste

DIRECTIONS

1. Place the chiles in a dry skillet and gently toast until it is fragrant and pliable. Place the chiles in a bowl of hot water and let them soak for 30 minutes.

2. Drain the chiles, place them in a blender, and add the tomatoes, onion, and garlic. Puree until smooth.

3. Season the salsa with salt and use as desired.

Pea & Parmesan Dip

Yield: 2 Cups
Active Time: 10 Minutes
Total Time: 20 Minutes

INGREDIENTS

Salt and pepper, to taste

3 cups peas

1 cup water

3 tablespoons pine nuts

1 cup freshly grated Parmesan cheese

1 garlic clove, minced

½ cup fresh mint leaves, chiffonade

DIRECTIONS

1. Bring water to a boil in a large saucepan. Add salt and the peas and cook until the peas are bright green and warmed through, about 2 minutes.

2. Transfer half of the peas to a food processor. Add the water, pine nuts, Parmesan, and garlic and blitz until pureed.

3. Place the puree in a serving dish, add the peas and mint, and fold to incorporate. Season the dip with salt and pepper and enjoy.

Tzatziki

INGREDIENTS

1 cucumber, grated

1 garlic clove, minced

1 teaspoon kosher salt

¾ cup plain full-fat
Greek yogurt

1 tablespoon chopped
fresh mint

DIRECTIONS

1. Place the cucumber, garlic, and salt in a mixing bowl and let it rest for 1 hour.

2. Strain the cucumber mixture and reserve the liquid. Place the cucumber mixture in a mixing bowl, add the yogurt and mint, and stir to combine.

3. Incorporate the reserved liquid 1 teaspoon at a time until the tzatziki has the desired texture and store in the refrigerator until ready to serve.

Sultana & Mango Chutney

Yield: 1 Cup
Active Time: 10 Minutes
Total Time: 20 Minutes

INGREDIENTS

1½ tablespoons extra-virgin olive oil

½ red onion, diced

½ teaspoon red pepper flakes

½ teaspoon curry powder

½ teaspoon grated fresh ginger

1 garlic clove, minced

⅓ cup red wine vinegar

½ cup mango jam

¼ cup sultanas (golden raisins)

⅓ cup water

DIRECTIONS

1. Place the olive oil in a large skillet and warm it over medium heat. When the oil starts to shimmer, add the onion, red pepper flakes, and curry powder and cook, stirring frequently, until the onion starts to soften, about 3 minutes.

2. Stir in the ginger and garlic, cook for 1 minute, and then add the remaining ingredients. Bring to a simmer and cook until the mixture has reduced. Transfer to a serving dish and serve warm or at room temperature.

Yield: 1 Cup

Active Time: 5 Minutes

Total Time: 5 Minutes

Romesco Sauce

INGREDIENTS

2 large red bell peppers, roasted

1 garlic clove, smashed

½ cup slivered almonds, toasted

¼ cup tomato puree

2 tablespoons chopped fresh parsley

2 tablespoons sherry vinegar

1 teaspoon smoked paprika

Salt and pepper, to taste

½ cup extra-virgin olive oil

DIRECTIONS

1. Place all of the ingredients, except for the olive oil, in a blender or food processor and pulse until the mixture is smooth.

2. Add the olive oil in a steady stream and blitz until emulsified. Season with salt and pepper and use immediately.

White Bean & Rosemary Spread

Yield: 2 Cups

Active Time: 5 Minutes

Total Time: 35 Minutes

INGREDIENTS

1 (14 oz.) can of cannellini beans, drained and rinsed

2 tablespoons extra-virgin olive oil

2 teaspoons balsamic vinegar

2 garlic cloves, minced

1 tablespoon chopped fresh rosemary

½ celery stalk, peeled and minced

Salt and pepper, to taste

2 pinches of red pepper flakes

DIRECTIONS

1. Place half of the beans in a bowl and mash them. Add the rest of the beans, the olive oil, vinegar, garlic, rosemary, and celery and stir to combine.

2. Season with salt, pepper, and red pepper flakes and cover the bowl with plastic wrap. Let stand for about 30 minutes before serving.

Roasted Pumpkin Dip

Yield: 6 to 8 Servings
Active Time: 5 Minutes
Total Time: 35 Minutes

INGREDIENTS

1 (3 lb.) sugar pumpkin, halved and seeds removed

5 tablespoons extra-virgin olive oil

2 teaspoons kosher salt

1 teaspoon black pepper

1 teaspoon chopped fresh thyme

¼ teaspoon freshly grated nutmeg

¼ cup grated Parmesan cheese

1 tablespoon fresh lemon juice

1 tablespoon plain full-fat Greek yogurt

DIRECTIONS

1. Preheat the oven to 425°F. Place the pumpkin, cut side up, on a parchment-lined baking sheet and brush it with 1 tablespoon of the olive oil. Sprinkle half of the salt over the pumpkin, turn it cut side down, and place it in the oven. Roast for 25 to 30 minutes, until the flesh is tender. Remove from the oven and let the pumpkin cool.

2. When the pumpkin is cool enough to handle, scrape the flesh into a food processor. Add the remaining ingredients and puree until smooth.

Cilantro Chutney

INGREDIENTS

1 bunch of fresh cilantro

¼ cup grated fresh coconut

15 fresh mint leaves

1 tablespoon minced chile pepper

1 garlic clove

1 teaspoon grated ginger

1 plum tomato, peeled, seeds removed, and chopped

1 tablespoon fresh lemon juice

Water, as needed

Salt, to taste

DIRECTIONS

1. Place all the ingredients, except for the water and salt, in a food processor and puree until smooth, adding water as needed to get the desired consistency. Season with salt and store in the refrigerator until ready to serve.

Beet Relish

INGREDIENTS

4 red beets, trimmed and rinsed well

1 large shallot, minced

2 teaspoons white wine vinegar

Salt and pepper, to taste

1 tablespoon red wine vinegar

2 tablespoons extra-virgin olive oil

DIRECTIONS

1. Preheat the oven to 400°F. Place the beets in a baking dish, add a splash of water, cover the dish with aluminum foil, and place it in the oven. Roast the beets until they are so tender that a knife easily goes to the center when poked, about 45 minutes. Remove from the oven, remove the foil, and let the beets cool.

2. While the beets are in the oven, place the shallot and white wine vinegar in a mixing bowl, season the mixture with salt, and stir to combine. Let the mixture rest.

3. Peel the beets, dice them, and place them in a mixing bowl. Add the remaining ingredients and the shallot mixture, season to taste, and serve.

Salads & Sides

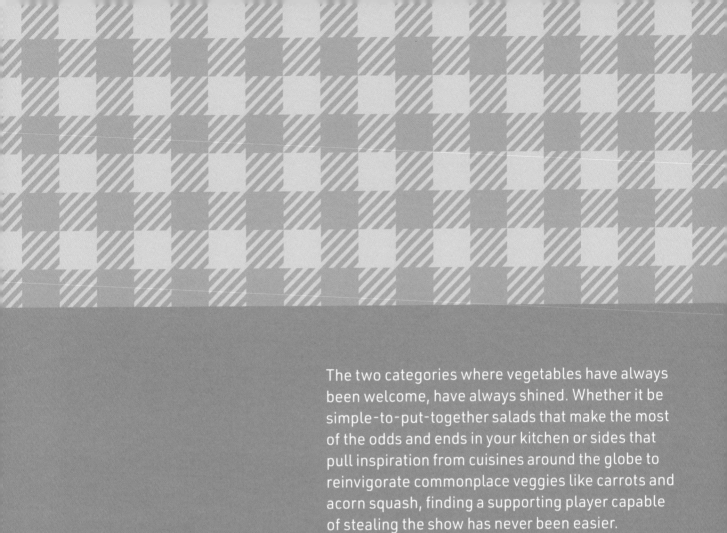

The two categories where vegetables have always been welcome, have always shined. Whether it be simple-to-put-together salads that make the most of the odds and ends in your kitchen or sides that pull inspiration from cuisines around the globe to reinvigorate commonplace veggies like carrots and acorn squash, finding a supporting player capable of stealing the show has never been easier.

Panzanella with White Balsamic Vinaigrette

Yield: 6 Servings
Active Time: 25 Minutes
Total Time: 45 Minutes

INGREDIENTS

For the Salad

1 tablespoon kosher salt, plus 2 teaspoons

6 pearl onions, trimmed

1 cup corn kernels

1 cup chopped green beans

4 cups chopped or torn day-old bread

2 cups chopped overripe tomatoes

10 large fresh basil leaves, torn

Black pepper, to taste

For the Vinaigrette

½ cup white balsamic vinegar

¼ cup extra-virgin olive oil

2 tablespoons minced shallot

¼ cup sliced scallions

2 tablespoons chopped fresh parsley

2 teaspoons kosher salt

1 teaspoon black pepper

DIRECTIONS

1. To begin preparations for the salad, bring water to a boil in a small saucepan and prepare an ice bath. When the water is boiling, add the 1 tablespoon of salt and the pearl onions and cook for 5 minutes. When the onions have 1 minute left to cook, add the corn and green beans to the saucepan. Transfer the vegetables to the ice bath and let cool completely.

2. Remove the pearl onions from the water bath and squeeze to remove the bulbs from their skins. Cut the bulbs in half and break them down into individual petals. Drain the corn and green beans and pat the vegetables dry.

3. To prepare the vinaigrette, place all the ingredients in a mixing bowl and whisk until combined.

4. Place the cooked vegetables, bread, tomatoes, and basil in a salad bowl and toss to combine. Add the remaining salt, season with pepper, and add half of the vinaigrette. Toss to coat, taste, and add more vinaigrette if desired.

Strawberry & Beet Salad

Yield: 4 Servings
Active Time: 20 Minutes
Total Time: 2 Hours

INGREDIENTS

3 large golden beets

½ cup extra-virgin olive oil

Salt and pepper, to taste

1 bunch of fresh cilantro, pureed

12 strawberries, hulls removed and halved

2 cups shredded queso fresco

4 oz. wild baby arugula

2 tablespoons annatto oil

DIRECTIONS

1. Preheat the oven to 375°F. Rinse the beets under cold water and scrub them to remove any excess dirt. Pat the beets dry and place them in a baking dish.

2. Drizzle the olive oil over the beets and season them generously with salt and pepper. Place them in the oven and roast until tender, about 1 hour.

3. Remove from the oven and let the beets cool.

4. When the beets are cool enough to handle, peel and dice them. Place them in a bowl with the cilantro and toss to coat. Add the strawberries, cheese, arugula, and annatto oil, toss until evenly distributed, and enjoy.

Ensalada de Nopales

Yield: 4 Servings
Active time: 30 minutes
Total time: 45 minutes

INGREDIENTS

3 large nopales (cactus), spines removed

1 tablespoon kosher salt, plus more to taste

½ white onion, finely chopped

2 large tomatoes, finely chopped

½ bunch of fresh cilantro, chopped

Juice of 1 lemon

Queso fresco, shredded, for garnish (optional)

Cotija cheese, crumbled, for garnish (optional)

DIRECTIONS

1. Place the nopales in a small bowl and sprinkle the salt all over them. Let rest for 15 minutes.

2. Combine the onion, tomatoes, and cilantro in a separate bowl.

3. Place the nopales and 1 tablespoon of water in a large skillet, cover it, and cook over medium heat until the nopales are tender, about 12 minutes. Remove from the pan and let cool. When cool enough to handle, cut into ¼-inch strips.

4. Stir the nopales into the tomato mixture, add the lemon juice, and season the salad with salt. If desired, sprinkle queso fresco or cotija cheese over the top.

Southwestern Rice Salad with Black Beans

Yield: 4 Servings
Active Time: 45 Minutes
Total Time: 45 Minutes

INGREDIENTS

For the Salad

1 cup long-grain white rice, rinsed

¾ cup cooked corn kernels

1¾ cups canned black beans, drained and rinsed

2 cups halved grape tomatoes

4 scallions, trimmed and sliced

Salt and pepper, to taste

Lime wedges, for serving

For the Dressing

Juice of 1 lime

Salt and pepper, to taste

¼ cup extra-virgin olive oil

1 red chile pepper, stems and seeds removed, minced

Handful of fresh cilantro, chopped

DIRECTIONS

1. To prepare the salad, bring 2 cups of lightly salted water to a boil in a medium saucepan. Add the rice, reduce the heat to low, cover with a lid, and cook for 15 to 20 minutes, or until water is absorbed and rice is tender. Remove from heat and let the rice cool, keeping the cover on.

2. Fluff the rice with a fork and transfer to a salad bowl. Add the corn, black beans, tomatoes, and scallions and stir to combine.

3. To prepare the dressing, place the lime juice in a bowl, season with salt and pepper, and add the olive oil in a slow, steady stream while whisking to incorporate. Stir in the chile and cilantro, taste, and adjust the seasoning as necessary.

4. Drizzle the dressing over the salad and gently toss to coat. Serve with lime wedges on the side.

Jerk Marinade

Place ¼ cup real maple syrup, ¼ cup lightly packed brown sugar, 1 tablespoon molasses, ½ teaspoon cayenne pepper, 1 teaspoon chili powder, 1 teaspoon paprika, 1 teaspoon cumin, ½ teaspoon ground cloves, 1 teaspoon cinnamon, ½ teaspoon nutmeg, 2 teaspoons kosher salt, 1 teaspoon black pepper, 2 teaspoons minced fresh ginger, 1 tablespoon finely chopped thyme, 2 tablespoons sliced scallions, 2 tablespoons chopped shallot, 1 tablespoon minced garlic, and 1 tablespoon fresh lime juice in a blender and puree until smooth.

Yield: 4 Servings
Active Time: 25 Minutes
Total Time: 2 Hours

Jerk Squash Salad

INGREDIENTS

For the Squash & Salad

2 acorn squash

Jerk Marinade (see sidebar)

1 tablespoon extra-virgin olive oil

½ teaspoon kosher salt

¼ teaspoon black pepper

¼ teaspoon paprika

6 cups baby kale

½ cup dried cranberries

1 cup crumbled feta cheese

For the Maple Vinaigrette

½ cup apple cider vinegar

½ cup real maple syrup

1 teaspoon orange zest

2 teaspoons Dijon mustard

1 tablespoon kosher salt

1 teaspoon black pepper

2 ice cubes

1½ cups extra-virgin olive oil

DIRECTIONS

1. Preheat the oven to 400°F. To begin preparations for the squash and salad, cut the squash in half lengthwise, remove the seeds, and reserve them. Trim the bottom of each half so that it can sit flat when cut-side up on a baking sheet. Score the flesh in a crosshatch pattern, cutting approximately ⅛ inch into the flesh. Brush some of the marinade on the squash and then fill the cavities with ⅓ cup. Place the baking sheet in the oven and bake until the squash is tender, about 45 minutes to 1 hour. As the squash is cooking, brush the flesh with the marinade in the cavities every 15 minutes. Remove from the oven and let cool. Lower the oven's temperature to 350°F.

2. Run the seeds under water and remove any pulp. Pat the seeds dry, place them in a mixing bowl, and add the olive oil, salt, pepper, and paprika. Toss to combine and then place the seeds on a baking sheet. Place in the oven and bake until they are light brown and crispy, about 7 minutes.

3. Place the toasted seeds, kale, and cranberries in a salad bowl and toss to combine.

4. To prepare the vinaigrette, place all the ingredients, except for the olive oil, in a blender. Turn on high and add the oil in a slow stream. Puree until the mixture has emulsified.

5. Add the vinaigrette to the salad bowl. Toss to coat evenly and top the salad with the crumbled feta. To serve, place a bed of salad on each plate and place one of the roasted halves of squash on top.

Chilled Corn Salad

Yield: 4 Servings
Active Time: 5 Minutes
Total Time: 3 Hours and 10 minutes

INGREDIENTS

4 cups cooked corn kernels

2 tablespoons unsalted butter

1 jalapeño chile pepper, stems and seeds removed, diced

2 tablespoons mayonnaise

2 teaspoons garlic powder

3 tablespoons sour cream

¼ teaspoon cayenne pepper

¼ teaspoon chili powder

2 tablespoons goat cheese

2 tablespoons cotija cheese

2 teaspoons fresh lime juice

½ cup finely chopped fresh cilantro

Salt and pepper, to taste

4 cups lettuce or arugula

DIRECTIONS

1. Place the corn in a large mixing bowl. Add all the remaining ingredients, except for the lettuce, and stir to combine.

2. Place the salad in the refrigerator and refrigerate for 3 hours. When ready to serve, add the lettuce and stir to incorporate.

Quinoa with Spinach, Mushrooms & Herbs

Yield: 6 Servings

Active Time: 20 Minutes

Total Time: 5 Hours

INGREDIENTS

1½ cups quinoa, rinsed

2½ cups Vegetable Stock (see page 119)

1 yellow onion, chopped

½ red bell pepper, stems and seeds removed, chopped

¾ lb. portobello mushrooms, chopped

2 garlic cloves, minced

1 tablespoon kosher salt, plus more to taste

1 tablespoon black pepper, plus more to taste

3 cups baby spinach

1½ cups fresh basil leaves, finely chopped

¼ cup finely chopped fresh dill

2 tablespoons finely chopped fresh thyme

DIRECTIONS

1. Place all the ingredients, except for the spinach and fresh herbs, in a slow cooker and cook on high until the quinoa is slightly fluffy, about 4 hours.

2. Add the spinach and turn off the heat. Keep the slow cooker covered and let sit for 1 hour.

3. Fluff the quinoa with a fork, add the basil, dill, and thyme, and fold to incorporate. Season with salt and pepper and serve.

Yield: 4 Servings

Active Time: 15 Minutes

Total Time: 15 Minutes

Spicy Broccolini

INGREDIENTS

½ lb. broccolini, trimmed

Salt and pepper, to taste

2 tablespoons extra-virgin olive oil

6 garlic cloves, minced

1½ tablespoons red wine vinegar

¼ teaspoon red pepper flakes, or to taste

Slivered almonds, toasted, for garnish

DIRECTIONS

1. Bring water to a boil in a large saucepan. Add salt until the water tastes like seawater. Add the broccolini and cook for 40 seconds. Drain and transfer the broccolini to a paper towel–lined plate.

2. Coat a skillet with olive oil and warm it over medium-high heat. When the oil starts to shimmer, add the broccolini and cook until well browned. Turn the broccolini over, season with salt and pepper, and cook until browned all over.

3. Stir in the garlic, vinegar, and red pepper flakes and cook, while tossing to combine, for another minute. Transfer to a serving platter and garnish with toasted almonds before serving.

Corn Tortillas

Yield: 32 Tortillas
Active Time: 30 Minutes
Total Time: 30 Minutes

INGREDIENTS

1 lb. masa harina

1½ tablespoons kosher salt

3 cups warm filtered water, plus more as needed

DIRECTIONS

1. In the work bowl of stand mixer fitted with the paddle attachment, combine the masa harina and salt. With the mixer on low speed, slowly begin to add the water. The mixture should come together as a soft, smooth dough. You want the mixture to be moist enough so that when a small ball of it is pressed flat in your hands the edges do not crack. Also, the mixture should not stick to your hands when you peel it off your palm.

2. Let the mixture rest for 10 minutes and check the hydration again. You may need to add more water depending on environmental conditions.

3. Warm a cast-iron skillet over high heat. Portion the mixture into 1-ounce balls and cover them with a damp linen towel.

4. Line a tortilla press with two 8-inch circles of plastic. You can use a grocery store bag, a resealable bag, or even a standard kitchen trash bag as a source for the plastic. Place the balls of masa in the center of one circle and gently push down on it with the palm of your hand to flatten. Place the other plastic circle on top and then close the tortilla press, applying firm, even pressure to flatten the masa into a round tortilla.

5. Open the tortilla press and remove the top layer of plastic. Carefully pick up the tortilla and carefully remove the bottom piece of plastic.

6. Gently lay the tortilla flat in the pan, taking care to not wrinkle it. Cook for 15 to 30 seconds, until the edges begin to lift up slightly. Turn the tortilla over and let it cook for 30 to 45 seconds before turning it over one last time. If the hydration was correct and the heat is high enough, the tortilla should puff up and inflate. Remove the tortilla from the pan and cover with a linen towel. Repeat until all of the balls have been made into tortillas.

Peperonata

INGREDIENTS

½ cup extra-virgin olive oil

4 large garlic cloves, sliced thin

1 red onion, halved and sliced

2 teaspoons kosher salt, plus more to taste

Black pepper, to taste

4 red bell peppers, stems and seeds removed, sliced thin

1 tablespoon sherry vinegar

1 tablespoon dried oregano

½ cup pitted black olives

Caper berries, drained, for garnish (optional)

DIRECTIONS

1. Place a rack in the middle position in the oven and preheat the oven to 400°F. Place the olive oil in a large skillet and warm it over medium-high heat. When the oil starts to shimmer, add the garlic and onion and cook, stirring frequently, until they begin to soften, about 1 minute.

2. Season with salt and pepper, add the bell peppers, and cook, stirring occasionally, until the peppers begin to soften, about 10 minutes.

3. Stir in the sherry vinegar and oregano and cook for another 2 minutes. Transfer the mixture to a large baking dish and use a wooden spoon to make sure it is distributed evenly.

4. Top with the olives, place the dish in the oven, and bake until the edges of the peperonata start to char, 1 to 1½ hours. Remove from the oven, top the peperonata with the caper berries (if desired), and serve.

Brussels Sprouts with Sherry Vinaigrette & Bread Crumbs

Yield: 4 Servings
Active Time: 15 Minutes
Total Time: 25 Minutes

INGREDIENTS

For the Vinaigrette

¼ cup sherry vinegar

2 tablespoons minced shallots

1 teaspoon kosher salt

½ teaspoon black pepper

2 tablespoons extra-virgin olive oil

For the Brussels Sprouts

½ cup extra-virgin olive oil, plus more as needed

1 lb. Brussels sprouts, trimmed and halved

1 tablespoon kosher salt

½ teaspoon black pepper

1 tablespoon fresh lemon juice

Fresh bread crumbs, toasted, for garnish

Fresh herbs, finely chopped, for garnish

DIRECTIONS

1. To prepare the vinaigrette, place the vinegar, shallots, salt, and pepper in a small bowl and whisk to combine. Let the mixture sit for 5 minutes before adding the olive oil in a slow, steady stream while whisking to incorporate.

2. To begin preparations for the Brussels sprouts, place the Brussels sprouts in a bowl, drizzle olive oil generously over them, and sprinkle the salt and pepper on top. Toss to combine and set the Brussels sprouts aside.

3. Coat the bottom of a large skillet with some of the olive oil and warm it over medium heat. When the oil starts to shimmer, add half of the Brussels sprouts and cook until golden brown on both sides, about 3 minutes per side. Transfer the Brussels sprouts to a bowl, add more of the olive oil, and warm it. Add the remaining Brussels sprouts, cook them until browned on both sides, and then transfer them to the bowl.

4. Add the lemon juice and vinaigrette to the bowl and toss to combine. Taste, adjust the seasoning as necessary, and top with the bread crumbs and fine chopped herbs such as tarragon, chives, and/or parsley.

Sautéed Radicchio with Chickpeas

Yield: 4 Servings
Active Time: 1 Hour
Total Time: 24 Hours

INGREDIENTS

⅔ cup dried chickpeas, soaked overnight

1 tablespoon extra-virgin olive oil

1 small head of radicchio, cored and sliced thin

1 shallot, minced

1 garlic clove, minced

¼ cup white wine

¼ cup Vegetable Stock (see page 119)

½ teaspoon finely chopped fresh thyme

Salt and pepper, to taste

Parmesan cheese, freshly grated, for garnish

Balsamic vinegar, to taste

DIRECTIONS

1. Drain the chickpeas. Place them in a large saucepan, cover with water, and bring to a gentle simmer. Reduce the heat so that the beans simmer and cook, stirring occasionally, until tender, about 2 hours. Drain and let the chickpeas cool.

2. Place the oil in a skillet and warm over medium heat. When the oil starts to shimmer, add the radicchio and cook, stirring frequently, until it starts to wilt and brown, about 5 minutes. Stir in the shallot and garlic and sauté until the garlic starts to brown, about 1 minute. Deglaze the pan with the wine and stock.

3. Add the chickpeas to the radicchio mixture along with the thyme. Season the mixture with salt and pepper, cook until almost all of the liquid has evaporated, and then remove the pan from heat. Top with Parmesan and balsamic vinegar and serve.

Sautéed Sunchokes

Yield: 4 to 6 Servings
Active Time: 15 Minutes
Total Time: 45 Minutes

INGREDIENTS

Salt and pepper, to taste

1½ lbs. sunchokes, peeled

¼ cup extra-virgin olive oil

1 garlic clove, minced

1 tablespoon chopped
fresh parsley

DIRECTIONS

1. Bring water to a boil in a large saucepan. Add salt and the sunchokes and parboil for 30 seconds. Drain and let them cool. When the sunchokes are cool enough to handle, slice them thin and pat dry with paper towels.

2. Place the olive oil in a large skillet and warm it over medium heat. When the oil starts to shimmer, add the garlic and cook, stirring constantly, for 1 minute. Add the sunchokes and parsley, season the mixture with salt and pepper, and cook, stirring occasionally, until the sunchokes are very tender, 10 to 15 minutes.

3. Taste, adjust the seasoning as needed, and enjoy.

Roasted Coffee & Ancho Carrots

Yield: 4 Servings

Active Time: 45 Minutes

Total Time: 45 Minutes

INGREDIENTS

1 bunch of organic carrots, leafy greens reserved for garnish

2 tablespoons extra-virgin olive oil

2 tablespoons instant coffee

2 tablespoons ancho chile powder

⅛ teaspoon coriander seeds, toasted and ground

1 tablespoon sumac powder

Salt, to taste

DIRECTIONS

1. Preheat the oven to 420°F. Place the carrots in a mixing bowl, add the olive oil, and toss to coat.

2. Combine the coffee, chili powder, toasted coriander, and sumac in a small bowl and then sprinkle the mixture over the carrots. Season with salt and toss until the carrots are evenly coated.

3. Place the carrots in a baking dish, place it in the oven, and roast the carrots until they are charred, cooked through, and al dente, 15 to 20 minutes. Remove from the oven and let the carrots cool slightly before enjoying.

Frijoles de la Olla

INGREDIENTS

1 cup dried beans, sorted, rinsed, and soaked overnight

1 white onion, quartered

3 garlic cloves

1 tablespoon white vinegar

Salt, to taste

5 sprigs of fresh epazote or cilantro

DIRECTIONS

1. Place 8 cups of water in a medium saucepan and bring it to a boil.

2. Add the beans, onion, garlic, and vinegar and cook until the beans are tender, about 1 hour and 30 minutes.

3. Remove a spoonful containing five beans from the pan and blow on them—if their skins peel back, they're ready.

4. Season with salt and the epazote and drain, making sure to reserve the broth.

Romano Beans with Mustard Vinaigrette & Walnuts

Yield: 8 Servings
Active Time: 15 Minutes
Total Time: 30 Minutes

INGREDIENTS

1 cup walnuts

Salt and pepper, to taste

3 lbs. Romano beans, trimmed

3 tablespoons red wine vinegar

2 tablespoons Dijon mustard

1 garlic clove, finely grated

2 tablespoons extra-virgin olive oil, plus more to taste

Zest of ½ lemon

¾ cup chopped fresh parsley

DIRECTIONS

1. Preheat the oven to 350°F. Place the walnuts on a rimmed baking sheet, place them in the oven, and toast until browned and fragrant, about 8 to 10 minutes, tossing halfway through. Remove the walnuts from the oven and let them cool. When the walnuts have cooled slightly, chop them and set aside.

2. Bring salted water to a boil in a large saucepan and prepare an ice bath. Place the beans in the boiling water and cook until bright green and tender, 8 to 10 minutes. Using a slotted spoon, transfer them to the ice bath and let them cool. Drain, pat the beans dry, and set them aside.

3. Place the vinegar, mustard, garlic, and olive oil in a large mixing bowl and stir until thoroughly combined. Let the dressing rest for 10 minutes.

4. Add the walnuts and beans to the dressing. Sprinkle the lemon zest and parsley over the beans, season with salt and pepper, and toss to coat. Transfer to a platter, drizzle more olive oil over the top, and enjoy.

NOTE: If Romano beans are not available, greens beans can be substituted.

Yield: 12 Servings
Active Time: 20 Minutes
Total Time: 1 Hour

Braised Leeks

INGREDIENTS

½ cup extra-virgin olive oil

6 large leeks, trimmed, rinsed well, and halved lengthwise

Salt and pepper, to taste

2 tablespoons avocado oil

4 shallots, chopped

2 garlic cloves, minced

1 teaspoon dried thyme

1 teaspoon lemon zest

2 cups Vegetable Stock (see page 119)

½ cup white wine

DIRECTIONS

1. Preheat the oven to 400°F. Place the olive oil in a large skillet and warm it over medium-high heat. Season the leeks with salt and pepper, place them in the pan, cut side down, and sear until golden brown, about 5 minutes.

2. Season the leeks with salt and pepper, turn them over, and cook until browned on that side, about 2 minutes. Transfer the leeks to a baking dish.

3. Place the avocado oil in the skillet and warm it over medium-high heat. Add the shallots and cook until they start to brown, about 5 minutes.

4. Add the garlic, thyme, lemon zest, salt, and pepper to the pan and cook until just fragrant, about 1 minute.

5. Add the wine and cook until it has reduced by half, about 10 minutes.

6. Add the stock and bring the mixture to a boil. Remove the pan from heat, and pour the mixture over the leeks until they are almost, but not quite, submerged.

7. Place the dish in the oven and braise the leeks until tender, about 30 minutes. Remove from the oven and enjoy.

Yield: 2 Servings
Active Time: 15 Minutes
Total Time: 4 Hours and
30 Minutes

Escabeche

INGREDIENTS

1 carrot, peeled and
sliced thin

1 cup cauliflower florets

1 radish, trimmed and
sliced thin

6 green beans, chopped

½ jalapeño chile pepper,
sliced thin

2 garlic cloves, smashed

1 ½ teaspoons sugar

½ teaspoon fine sea salt

½ teaspoon peppercorns

½ cup distilled white
vinegar

1 cup water

DIRECTIONS

1. Layer the vegetables in a sterilized mason jar.

2. Place the remaining ingredients in a saucepan and bring to a boil over medium-high heat, stirring to dissolve the sugar. Pour the brine over the vegetables and let it cool to room temperature.

3. Cover the jar and chill it in the refrigerator for at least 4 hours before serving.

Smoked Sweet Potato Puree

Yield: 8 Servings

Active Time: 15 Minutes

Total Time: 1 Hour and 15 Minutes

INGREDIENTS

½ cup wood chips

2 sweet potatoes, peeled and chopped

1 Yukon Gold potato, peeled and chopped

2 teaspoons kosher salt, plus more to taste

½ cup heavy cream

2 tablespoons unsalted butter

DIRECTIONS

1. Preheat the oven to 250°F. Place the wood chips in a cast-iron skillet and place the pan over high heat. When the wood chips start to smoke, place the skillet in a deep roasting pan. Set the sweet potatoes and potato in the roasting pan (not in the skillet) and cover the roasting pan with aluminum foil. Place in the oven for 30 minutes.

2. While the potatoes are smoking in the oven, bring water to a boil in a large saucepan. Remove the potatoes from the oven, salt the boiling water, and add the potatoes. Cook until they are fork-tender, 20 to 25 minutes. Drain, place in a mixing bowl, and add the remaining ingredients. Mash until smooth and serve immediately.

Cornbread

INGREDIENTS

½ cup honey

12 oz. unsalted butter, softened

1 lb. all-purpose flour

8 oz. cornmeal

1 tablespoon baking powder, plus 1 teaspoon

1 tablespoon kosher salt

7 oz. sugar

4 eggs

2 cups milk

DIRECTIONS

1. Preheat the oven to 350°F. Coat a 13 x 9-inch baking pan with nonstick cooking spray.

2. Place the honey and 4 oz. of the butter in a small saucepan and warm over medium heat until the butter has melted. Whisk to combine and set the mixture aside.

3. Place the flour, cornmeal, baking powder, and salt in a mixing bowl and whisk to combine. Set the mixture aside.

4. In the work bowl of a stand mixer fitted with the paddle attachment, cream the remaining butter and the sugar on medium until light and fluffy, about 5 minutes. Add the eggs and beat until incorporated. Add the dry mixture, reduce the speed to low, and beat until the mixture comes together as a smooth batter. Gradually add the milk and beat until incorporated.

5. Pour the batter into the pan, place the pan in the oven, and bake until a cake tester inserted in the center of the cornbread comes out clean, 25 to 30 minutes.

6. Remove from the oven and place the pan on a wire rack. Brush the cornbread with the honey butter and serve it warm.

Soups

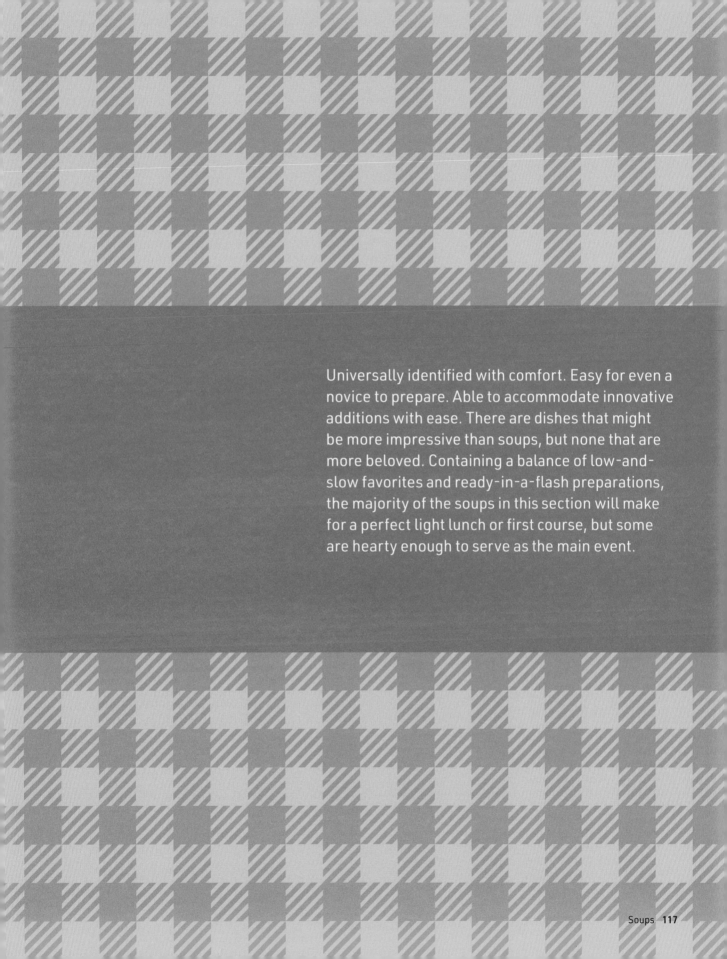

Universally identified with comfort. Easy for even a novice to prepare. Able to accommodate innovative additions with ease. There are dishes that might be more impressive than soups, but none that are more beloved. Containing a balance of low-and-slow favorites and ready-in-a-flash preparations, the majority of the soups in this section will make for a perfect light lunch or first course, but some are hearty enough to serve as the main event.

Vegetable Stock

Yield: 6 Cups
Active Time: 20 Minutes
Total Time: 3 Hours

INGREDIENTS

2 tablespoons olive oil

2 large leeks, trimmed and rinsed well

2 large carrots, peeled and sliced

2 celery stalks, sliced

2 large yellow onions, sliced

3 garlic cloves, unpeeled but smashed

2 sprigs of parsley

2 sprigs of thyme

1 bay leaf

8 cups water

½ teaspoon black peppercorns

Salt, to taste

DIRECTIONS

1. Place the olive oil and the vegetables in a large stockpot and cook over low heat until the liquid they release has evaporated. This will allow the flavor of the vegetables to become concentrated.

2. Add the garlic, parsley, thyme, bay leaf, water, peppercorns, and salt. Raise the heat to high and bring to a boil. Reduce heat so that the stock simmers and cook for 2 hours, while skimming to remove any impurities that float to the top.

3. Strain through a fine sieve, let the stock cool slightly, and place in the refrigerator, uncovered, to chill. Remove the fat layer and cover. The stock will keep in the refrigerator for 3 to 5 days, and in the freezer for up to 3 months.

Ribollita

Yield: 4 Servings
Active Time: 30 Minutes
Total Time: 1 Hour and 30 Minutes

INGREDIENTS

5 tablespoons extra-virgin olive oil

1 small yellow onion, chopped

1 carrot, peeled and chopped

1 celery stalk, peeled and chopped

2 garlic cloves, minced

Salt and pepper, to taste

2 cups canned cannellini beans, rinsed well

1 lb. canned, whole, and peeled San Marzano tomatoes, with their juices, crushed by hand

4 cups Vegetable Stock (see page 119)

1 sprig of fresh rosemary

1 sprig of fresh thyme

1 lb. kale or escarole, chopped

4 large, thick slices of day-old bread, toasted

1 small red onion, sliced thin

½ cup freshly grated Parmesan cheese

DIRECTIONS

1. Place 2 tablespoons of the oil in a large saucepan and warm it over medium heat. When the oil starts to shimmer, add the onion, carrot, celery, and garlic, season the mixture with salt and pepper, and cook, stirring occasionally, until the vegetables are soft, about 10 minutes.

2. Preheat the oven to 500°F. Add the beans to the pot along with the tomatoes and their juices, stock, rosemary, and thyme. Bring to a boil, reduce the heat so the soup simmers, and cover the pan. Cook, stirring occasionally, until the flavors have developed, 15 to 20 minutes.

3. Remove the rosemary and thyme and discard. Stir in the kale, taste the soup, and adjust the seasoning if necessary. Lay the bread slices on top of the stew so they cover as much of the surface as possible. Sprinkle the red onion and Parmesan on top and drizzle the remaining olive oil over everything.

4. Place the pan in the oven and bake until the bread, onions, and cheese are browned and crisp, 10 to 15 minutes. Ladle the soup and bread into warmed bowls and serve.

Quick & Easy Minestrone

Yield: 4 Servings

Active Time: 30 Minutes

Total Time: 1 Hour and 15 Minutes

INGREDIENTS

2 tablespoons extra-virgin olive oil

1 garlic clove, minced

2 onions, minced

2 carrots, peeled and minced

1 leek, white part only, rinsed well and minced

2 yellow bell peppers, stems and seeds removed, minced

2 red bell peppers, stems and seeds removed, minced

2 zucchini, minced

8 cherry tomatoes, chopped

6 cups tomato juice

½ teaspoon chopped fresh thyme

½ teaspoon chopped fresh rosemary

Salt and pepper, to taste

Parmesan cheese, shaved, for garnish

DIRECTIONS

1. Place the oil in a large saucepan and warm it over medium heat. Add the garlic, onions, carrots, and leek and cook, stirring frequently, until the vegetables start to soften, about 5 minutes.

2. Add the peppers, cook for 5 minutes, and then stir in the zucchini and cherry tomatoes. Cook for 3 minutes, add the tomato juice, thyme, and rosemary, and bring to a boil.

3. Reduce the heat so that the soup simmers and cook until the vegetables are tender, about 20 minutes. Season with salt and pepper, ladle into warmed bowls, and garnish with the Parmesan.

Tomato Soup with Chickpeas & Pasta

Yield: 4 Servings

Active Time: 20 Minutes

Total Time: 35 Minutes

INGREDIENTS

2 tablespoons extra-virgin olive oil

1 onion, chopped

2 garlic cloves, minced

2 (28 oz.) cans of whole tomatoes, pureed

2 tablespoons finely chopped fresh thyme

4 cups Vegetable Stock (see page 119)

½ cup pasta, such as ditalini or orecchiette

1 (14 oz.) can of chickpeas, drained and rinsed

¼ cup chopped fresh parsley

¼ cup freshly grated Parmesan cheese, plus more for garnish

Salt and pepper, to taste

Fresh basil, chopped, for garnish

DIRECTIONS

1. Place the olive oil in a large saucepan and warm over medium heat. When the oil starts to shimmer, add the onion and sauté until it starts to soften, about 5 minutes. Add the garlic, cook for 1 minute, and then stir in the pureed tomatoes, thyme, and stock.

2. Bring the soup to a boil, reduce the heat so that the soup simmers, and add the pasta. Cook until it is tender, about 8 minutes.

3. Stir in the chickpeas, parsley, and Parmesan and cook for 3 minutes. Season with salt and pepper, ladle into warmed bowls, and garnish with additional Parmesan and the basil.

Buttermilk Stew with Spinach Dumplings

Yield: 6 to 8 Servings
Active Time: 15 Minutes
Total Time: 30 Minutes

INGREDIENTS

For the Stew

8 cups buttermilk

½ cup chickpea flour

1 tablespoon turmeric

1 teaspoon kosher salt

1 tablespoon extra-virgin olive oil

1 teaspoon coriander seeds

1 tablespoon black mustard seeds

2 large yellow onions, sliced into thin half-moons

6 garlic cloves, minced

2-inch piece of fresh ginger, peeled and grated

1 teaspoon amchoor powder

2 serrano chile peppers, stems and seeds removed, minced

For the Dumplings

2 cups spinach, blanched and chopped

2 serrano chile peppers, stems and seeds removed, minced (optional)

2 teaspoons kosher salt

1 teaspoon red pepper flakes

1½ teaspoons chaat masala

1 cup chickpea flour

DIRECTIONS

1. To begin preparations for the stew, place half of the buttermilk, the chickpea flour, turmeric, and salt in a blender and puree until smooth. Set the mixture aside.

2. Place the oil in a Dutch oven and warm it over high heat. When the oil is shimmering, add the coriander and mustard seeds and cook, stirring constantly, until they start to pop, about 2 minutes.

3. Reduce the heat to medium and add the onions, garlic, ginger, amchoor powder, and chiles. Sauté until slightly browned and then pour in the buttermilk mixture. Add the remaining buttermilk, reduce the heat so that the stew gently simmers, and prepare the dumplings.

4. To prepare the dumplings, place the spinach, serrano peppers (if using), salt, red pepper flakes, and chaat masala in a mixing bowl and stir to combine. Add the chickpea flour and stir to incorporate. The dough should be quite stiff.

5. Add tablespoons of the dough to the stew. When all of the dumplings have been added, cover the Dutch oven and simmer over low heat until the dumplings are cooked through, about 10 minutes. Ladle into warmed bowls and serve.

NOTE: Amchoor is a sour powder made from the dried flesh of an unripe mango. Crucial to North Indian cuisine, you can find it at better grocery stores or online.

Borscht

INGREDIENTS

2 tablespoons extra-virgin olive oil

1 lb. beets, peeled and grated

1 onion, grated

2 garlic cloves, grated

1 lb. red cabbage, grated

1 large celery stalk, peeled and grated

2 carrots, peeled and grated

1 teaspoon fennel seeds

4 cups Vegetable Stock (see page 119), plus more as needed

2 tablespoons apple cider vinegar

1 tablespoon sugar

1 bay leaf

Salt and pepper, to taste

Sour cream, for garnish

DIRECTIONS

1. Place the olive oil in a medium saucepan and warm it over medium heat. Add the beets to the pan and cook, stirring occasionally, until they start to soften, about 8 minutes.

2. Add the onion and garlic and cook, stirring frequently, until the onion turns translucent, about 3 minutes. Add the cabbage, celery, carrots, and fennel seeds and cook until the vegetables start to become tender, about 10 minutes.

3. Add the stock, vinegar, sugar, and bay leaf. Make sure there is enough liquid to cover all of the ingredients; add more stock if needed. Simmer until all of the vegetables are tender, about 15 minutes. Season to taste, discard the bay leaf, and ladle the soup into warmed bowls. Top each portion with a dollop of sour cream.

Caramelized Onion Soup

Yield: 4 Servings
Active Time: 30 Minutes
Total Time: 1 Hour

INGREDIENTS

4 tablespoons unsalted butter

6 Spanish onions, chopped

2 garlic cloves, minced

½ teaspoon fresh thyme

½ cup Riesling

½ cup vermouth

4 cups heavy cream

Salt and pepper, to taste

Croutons, for garnish

DIRECTIONS

1. Place the butter in a medium saucepan and melt it over low heat. Add the onions, reduce the heat to the lowest possible setting, and cook until golden brown, about 30 minutes. Stir the onions every few minutes and add a bit of water whenever they begin to stick to the pan.

2. Add the garlic, thyme, Riesling, and vermouth and cook until the liquid has reduced by half. Add the cream and simmer for 10 minutes.

3. Transfer the soup to a food processor or blender and puree until smooth. Season the soup with salt and pepper, pour it into warmed bowls, and top each portion with croutons.

Yield: 4 Servings

Active Time: 20 Minutes

Total Time: 1 Hour

Mulligatawny

INGREDIENTS

4 teaspoons poppy seeds

½ teaspoon cumin seeds

1 teaspoon coriander seeds

¼ teaspoon turmeric

1 yellow onion, chopped

4 garlic cloves, minced

1-inch piece of fresh ginger,
peeled and grated

¼ cup extra-virgin olive oil

Pinch of cayenne pepper

4 cups Vegetable Stock
(see page 119)

¼ cup long-grain rice

1 tablespoon fresh lemon
juice

¼ cup coconut milk

Salt and pepper, to taste

Shredded coconut,
for garnish

Fresh cilantro, chopped,
for garnish

DIRECTIONS

1. Place the poppy seeds, cumin seeds, and coriander seeds in a dry skillet and toast for 30 seconds over medium heat. Place the toasted seeds, turmeric, onion, garlic, ginger, and 2 tablespoons of the oil in a food processor and blitz until the mixture is a paste. Set the mixture aside.

2. Place the remaining oil in a saucepan and warm it over medium-high heat. Add the paste and cook for 2 minutes, stirring constantly.

3. Stir in the cayenne pepper and stock and bring the soup to a boil. Reduce heat so that the soup simmers, add the rice, and cook until the rice is tender, about 20 minutes.

4. Stir in the lemon juice and coconut milk, season with salt and pepper, and ladle the soup into warmed bowls. Garnish with the coconut and cilantro and serve.

Spicy Carrot, Spinach & Tofu Soup

Yield: 4 Servings
Active Time: 20 Minutes
Total Time: 45 Minutes

INGREDIENTS

1 tablespoon extra-virgin olive oil

1 onion, chopped

1 red bell pepper, stems and seeds removed, chopped

2 tablespoons curry powder

1 garlic clove, minced

6 cups Vegetable Stock (see page 119)

1 chile pepper, stems and seeds removed, sliced

Zest and juice of 1 lime

2 tablespoons soy sauce

¼ cup packed brown sugar

1 carrot, peeled and sliced

2 cups spinach

1 zucchini, sliced thin

¾ lb. tofu, cut into ½-inch cubes

DIRECTIONS

1. Place the oil in a medium saucepan and warm it over medium heat. When the oil starts to shimmer, add the onion, pepper, and curry powder and cook, stirring frequently, until the onion and pepper start to soften, about 5 minutes.

2. Add the garlic and cook, while stirring, for 1 minute. Add the stock, chili pepper, lime zest and juice, soy sauce, brown sugar, and carrot. Bring to a boil, reduce the heat so that the soup simmers, and cook for 10 minutes.

3. Add the zucchini and continue to simmer for 5 minutes.

4. Just before serving, add the spinach and tofu. Cook until warmed through, season with salt and pepper, ladle into warmed bowls, and serve with the Naan.

Creamed Parsnip Soup

Yield: 4 Servings
Active Time: 15 Minutes
Total Time: 30 Minutes

INGREDIENTS

2 tablespoons unsalted butter

1 onion, chopped

1 garlic clove, minced

1 teaspoon fresh thyme

5 parsnips, trimmed, peeled, and grated

6 cups Vegetable Stock (see page 119)

2 cups heavy cream

Salt and pepper, to taste

Dried apples, for garnish

Parsley, chopped, for garnish

DIRECTIONS

1. Place the butter in a medium saucepan and melt over medium heat. Add the onion, garlic, and thyme and cook, stirring frequently, until the onion is soft, about 5 minutes.

2. Add the parsnips and cook for 5 minutes. Add the stock, bring the soup to a boil, and then reduce the heat so that it simmers. Cook until the parsnips are tender, about 10 minutes.

3. Remove the pan from heat and transfer the soup to a food processor or a blender. Puree until smooth and then strain through a fine sieve.

4. Return to the soup to a clean saucepan, bring to a simmer, and stir in the heavy cream. Simmer for 5 minutes.

5. Season the soup with salt and pepper, ladle it into warmed bowls, and garnish each portion with dried apples and parsley.

NOTE: If the parsnips are going to be sitting around for a bit after you grate them, leave them in cold water with a splash of lemon juice so that they don't oxidize.

Go for the Green Stew

Yield: 4 Servings
Active Time: 30 Minutes
Total Time: 1 Hour

INGREDIENTS

1 tablespoon extra-virgin olive oil

1 onion, chopped

2 garlic cloves, minced

1 celery stalk, peeled and minced

1 green bell pepper, stems and seeds removed, chopped

¼ head of green cabbage, cored and sliced thin

½ teaspoon chopped fresh marjoram

½ teaspoon fresh thyme

1 bay leaf

6 cups Vegetable Stock (see page 119)

2 cups shredded collard greens

2 cups shredded baby spinach

12 oz. tofu, drained and chopped into ¼-inch pieces

¼ cup fresh parsley, chopped

½ teaspoon allspice

Cayenne pepper, or to taste

Salt and pepper, to taste

DIRECTIONS

1. Place the olive oil in a large saucepan and warm over medium heat. Add the onion, garlic, celery, and bell pepper and sauté until the onion and celery start to soften, about 5 minutes.

2. Stir in the cabbage, marjoram, thyme, and bay leaf, cook for 5 minutes, and then add the stock. Bring the stew to a boil, reduce heat so that it simmers, and cook for 5 minutes.

3. Stir in the collard greens and cook for 5 minutes. Add the spinach and tofu and cook for 2 minutes before adding the parsley, allspice, and cayenne. Season with salt and pepper, simmer for 2 more minutes, and ladle into warmed bowls.

Asparagus & Pea Soup

Yield: 6 Servings
Active Time: 25 Minutes
Total Time: 1 Hour

INGREDIENTS

¾ lb. asparagus

2 tablespoons unsalted butter

1 leek, trimmed, rinsed well, and chopped

1¼ cups peas, ¼ cup reserved for garnish

1 tablespoon chopped fresh parsley

5 cups Vegetable Stock (see page 119)

½ cup heavy cream

Zest of 2 lemons, half reserved for garnish

Salt and pepper, to taste

Fresh mint leaves, for garnish

Parmesan cheese, shaved, for garnish

DIRECTIONS

1. Remove the woody ends of the asparagus and discard. Separate the spears, remove the tips, reserve them for garnish, and chop what remains into 1-inch-long pieces.

2. Place the butter in a saucepan and melt it over medium heat. Add the leek and cook, stirring frequently, until it starts to soften, about 5 minutes.

3. Add the chopped asparagus, the cup of peas, and the parsley. Cook for 3 minutes, stir in the stock, and bring to a boil. Reduce the heat so that the soup simmers and cook until the vegetables are tender, 6 to 8 minutes.

4. Transfer the soup to a food processor, puree until smooth, and strain through a fine sieve.

5. Place the soup in a clean saucepan. Add the cream and lemon zest, season with salt and pepper, and bring to a simmer.

6. Bring a small pan of salted water to a boil and prepare an ice water bath. Place the asparagus tips in the pan and cook for 3 to 4 minutes, or until tender. Remove the tips, submerge in the ice water bath, pat dry with paper towels, and set aside.

7. Ladle the soup into warmed bowls and garnish with the asparagus tips, reserved peas, mint leaves, reserved lemon zest, and Parmesan.

Rutabaga & Fig Soup

Yield: 4 Servings
Active Time: 20 Minutes
Total Time: 1 Hour

INGREDIENTS

2 tablespoons extra-virgin olive oil

1 onion, chopped

4 cups peeled and chopped rutabaga

1 tablespoon honey

4 cups Vegetable Stock (see page 119)

1 teaspoon fresh thyme

16 Black Mission figs

1 cup buttermilk

1 (14 oz.) can of chickpeas, drained and rinsed

1 teaspoon garam masala

Salt and pepper, to taste

DIRECTIONS

1. Place the olive oil in a medium saucepan and warm it over medium heat. Add the onion and rutabaga and cook, stirring frequently, until the onion is soft, about 10 minutes. Stir in the honey, stock, thyme, and figs and bring the soup to a boil.

2. Reduce the heat so that the soup simmers and cook until the rutabaga is tender, about 20 minutes.

3. Transfer the soup to a food processor or blender and puree until smooth. Return the soup to a clean pan, add the buttermilk, chickpeas, and garam masala, and bring to a simmer. Cook until everything is warmed through, about 5 minutes.

4. Season the soup with salt and pepper, ladle into warm bowls, and serve.

Entrees

Skeptics of the plant-based diet have long argued that when the main course rolls around, an approach limited to vegetables cannot consistently produce a dish as flavorful, filling, and exciting as one that makes use of everything available to omnivore. Luckily, you can let these dishes do the talking for you, and put that debate to rest.

Sweet & Spicy Roasted Barley

Yield: 4 Servings
Active Time: 20 Minutes
Total Time: 1 Hour and 30 Minutes

INGREDIENTS

5 carrots, peeled and cut into 3-inch pieces

Olive oil, to taste

Salt and pepper, to taste

6 pasilla chile peppers

2¼ cups boiling water

1 cup pearl barley

1 red onion, minced

2 tablespoons adobo seasoning

1 tablespoon sugar

1 tablespoon chili powder

¼ cup chopped fresh oregano

DIRECTIONS

1. Preheat the oven to 375°F. Place the carrots in a 13 x 9–inch baking dish, drizzle the olive oil over them, and season with salt and pepper. Place in the oven and roast until the carrots are slightly soft to the touch, about 45 minutes.

2. While the carrots are cooking, open the pasilla peppers and discard the seeds and stems. Place the peppers in a bowl, add the boiling water, and cover the bowl with aluminum foil.

3. When the carrots are cooked, remove the pan from the oven and add the remaining ingredients along with the liquid the peppers have been soaking in. Chop the reconstituted peppers, add them to the pan, and spread the mixture so that the liquid is covering the barley. Cover the pan tightly with aluminum foil, place it in the oven, and bake until the barley is tender, about 45 minutes. Fluff with a fork and serve immediately.

Spinach Frittata with Cherry Tomatoes

Yield: 4 Servings
Active Time: 20 Minutes
Total Time: 1 Hour and 10 Minutes

INGREDIENTS

Salt and pepper, to taste

1½ cups frozen spinach

2½ cups peeled and cubed potatoes

3 tablespoons extra-virgin olive oil

2 scallions, trimmed and chopped

1 garlic clove, chopped

6 eggs

Pinch of freshly grated nutmeg

1 cup halved cherry tomatoes

DIRECTIONS

1. Preheat the oven to 325°F. Thaw and drain the spinach. Bring salted water to a boil in a large saucepan.

2. Add the potatoes to the boiling water and cook until almost fork-tender, about 15 minutes. Drain and set the potatoes aside.

3. Place the olive oil in a skillet and warm it over medium heat. Add the scallions and garlic and cook, stirring frequently, until fragrant, about 2 minutes. Add the potatoes and cook, stirring frequently, for 2 minutes. Transfer the contents of the pan to a square baking dish.

4. Place the eggs in a large bowl and whisk until scrambled. Add the thawed spinach and nutmeg, season with salt and pepper, and pour the mixture into the baking dish.

5. Distribute the cherry tomatoes on top, place the dish in the oven, and bake until they eggs have set, about 30 minutes.

6. Remove from the oven and enjoy.

Pumpkin Curry

INGREDIENTS

1 ⅓ cups coconut milk

1 cup water, plus more
as needed

1 teaspoon turmeric

1 teaspoon curry powder

1-inch piece of fresh ginger,
peeled and grated

2 to 3 kaffir lime leaves

2 red or green chile
peppers, stems and seeds
removed, diced

2 garlic cloves, minced

1 tablespoon extra-virgin
olive oil

4 cups peeled and cubed
pumpkin

1 large onion, diced

Salt, to taste

1½ cups cooked white rice

DIRECTIONS

1. In a medium bowl, combine the coconut milk, water, turmeric, curry, ginger, lime leaves, chile peppers, and garlic.

2. Place the oil in a large skillet and warm it over medium heat. Add the cubed pumpkin and onion and sauté until the onion starts to soften. Add the coconut milk mixture and bring to a boil. Reduce heat and simmer until the pumpkin is fork-tender, about 20 minutes. If the pan starts looking to dry, add water, ¼ cup at a time.

3. Remove the skillet from heat and let it stand for 2 to 3 minutes. Season to taste with salt and serve over white rice.

Kung Pao Cauliflower

Yield: 4 Servings
Active Time: 30 Minutes
Total Time: 45 Minutes

INGREDIENTS

2 tablespoons dry sherry

2 tablespoons gluten-free dark soy sauce

1 tablespoon cornstarch

2 tablespoons sherry vinegar

2 tablespoons hoisin sauce

2 teaspoons coconut sugar

1½ teaspoons toasted sesame oil

3 tablespoons Vegetable Stock (see page 119)

2 tablespoons canola oil

1 head of cauliflower

Salt and pepper, to taste

½ red bell pepper, stems and seeds removed, sliced

2 jalapeño chile peppers, stems and seeds removed, sliced thin

2 red chile peppers, stems and seeds removed, sliced thin

1 teaspoon Sichuan peppercorns

1-inch piece of fresh ginger, peeled and grated

3 garlic cloves, minced

2 to 3 tablespoons salted peanuts, crushed, for garnish

2 scallions, trimmed and sliced on a bias, for garnish

1½ cups cooked white rice, for serving

DIRECTIONS

1. Place the sherry, half of the soy sauce, and the cornstarch in a large mixing bowl and stir to combine. Set the mixture aside.

2. Place the remaining soy sauce, sherry vinegar, hoisin sauce, coconut sugar, sesame oil, and stock in a separate bowl and whisk until the sugar has dissolved. Set the mixture aside.

3. Trim the cauliflower and cut it into large florets.

4. Place half of the oil in a wok or large cast-iron skillet and warm it over medium-high heat. Add the cauliflower to the pan in batches, season each addition with salt and pepper, and cook until lightly browned all over, about 8 minutes, turning it as necessary.

5. Stir the sherry-and-cornstarch marinade, add the cauliflower to it, and gently stir to coat.

6. Warm the remaining oil in the pan over medium heat. Add the bell pepper, jalapeño, red chiles, and peppercorns and stir-fry for 1 minute. Return the cauliflower to the pan, season it with salt, and cook until lightly charred all over and fork-tender, 6 to 8 minutes.

7. Stir in the ginger, garlic, and hoisin mixture. Bring the mixture to a boil and cook, stirring occasionally, until it has thickened.

8. Garnish with the peanuts and scallions and serve with white rice.

Mushroom & Chard Shepherd's Pie

Yield: 4 to 6 Servings

Active Time: 45 Minutes

Total Time: 1 Hour and 30 Minutes

INGREDIENTS

6 russet potatoes, peeled and chopped

½ teaspoon kosher salt, plus more to taste

11 tablespoons unsalted butter, cubed

½ cup milk

¼ cup plain yogurt

Black pepper, to taste

1 small onion, minced

3 cups chopped mushrooms

1 bunch of Swiss chard, rinsed well, leaves and stems separated, chopped

1 tablespoon soy sauce

Extra-virgin olive oil, as needed

DIRECTIONS

1. Preheat the oven to 350°F. Place the potatoes in a large saucepan, cover with cold water, and add the salt. Bring the water to a boil, reduce to a simmer, and cook the potatoes until they are fork-tender, about 20 minutes.

2. Drain the potatoes and place them in a large bowl. Add 6 tablespoons of the butter, the milk, and the yogurt and mash the potatoes until smooth and creamy. Season with salt and pepper and set aside.

3. In a large cast-iron skillet, melt 3 tablespoons of the butter over medium heat. Add the onion and cook until translucent, about 3 minutes. Add the mushrooms, the chard stems, and the soy sauce. Cook for about 3 minutes, stirring frequently, then reduce the heat to low and continue to cook until the mushrooms and chard stems are soft, another 5 minutes. If the pan seems dry, add a tablespoon of olive oil.

4. Increase the heat to medium and add the chard leaves. Cook, while stirring constantly, until the leaves wilt, about 3 minutes. Remove the skillet from heat and season with salt and pepper.

5. Spread the mashed potatoes over the mixture, distributing the potatoes evenly and smoothing the top with a rubber spatula. Cut the remaining 2 tablespoons of butter into slivers and dot the potatoes with them.

6. Cover with foil and bake for 25 minutes. Remove the foil and bake for another 10 minutes, until the topping is just browned and the filling is bubbly. Remove and briefly let cool before serving.

Yield: 4 Servings
Active Time: 15 Minutes
Total Time: 45 Minutes

Veggie Burgers

INGREDIENTS

1 (14 oz.) can black beans, drained and rinsed

⅓ cup minced scallions

¼ cup chopped roasted red peppers

¼ cup cooked corn kernels

½ cup panko

1 egg, lightly beaten

2 tablespoons chopped fresh cilantro

½ teaspoon cumin

½ teaspoon cayenne pepper

½ teaspoon black pepper

1 teaspoon fresh lime juice

1 tablespoon extra-virgin olive oil

Hamburger buns, for serving

Sweet Corn & Pepita Guacamole (see page 49), for serving

DIRECTIONS

1. Place half of the beans, the scallions, and roasted red peppers in a food processor and pulse until the mixture is a thick paste. Transfer to a large bowl.

2. Add the corn, bread crumbs, egg, cilantro, cumin, cayenne, black pepper, and lime juice to the bowl and stir to combine. Add the remaining beans and stir vigorously until the mixture holds together. Cover the bowl with plastic wrap and let it sit at room temperature for 30 minutes.

3. Place a large cast-iron skillet over medium-high heat and coat the bottom with the olive oil. Form the mixture into four patties, add them to the skillet, cover the pan, and cook until browned and cooked through, about 5 minutes per side. Serve immediately on hamburger buns with the Guacamole.

Ratatouille

Yield: 4 Servings
Active Time: 40 Minutes
Total Time: 2 Hours

INGREDIENTS

⅓ cup extra-virgin olive oil

6 garlic cloves, minced

1 eggplant, chopped

2 zucchini, sliced into half-moons

2 bell peppers, stems and seeds removed, and chopped

4 tomatoes, seeds removed, chopped

Salt and pepper, to taste

DIRECTIONS

1. Place a large cast-iron skillet over medium-high heat and add half of the olive oil. When the oil starts to shimmer, add the garlic and eggplant and cook, while stirring, until pieces are coated with oil and just starting to sizzle, about 2 minutes.

2. Reduce the heat to medium, add the zucchini, peppers, and remaining oil, and stir to combine. Cover the skillet and cook, stirring occasionally, until the eggplant, zucchini, and peppers are almost tender, about 15 minutes.

3. Add the tomatoes, stir to combine, and cook until the eggplant, zucchini, and peppers are tender and the tomatoes have collapsed, about 25 minutes. Remove the skillet from heat, season with salt and pepper, and allow to sit for at least 1 hour. Reheat before serving.

Green Bean & Tofu Casserole

Yield: 4 Servings
Active Time: 5 Minutes
Total Time: 2 Days

INGREDIENTS

For the Marinade

3 tablespoons soy sauce

2 tablespoons rice vinegar

1 tablespoon sesame oil

1 tablespoon honey

Pinch of cinnamon

Pinch of black pepper

For the Casserole

1 lb. extra-firm tofu, drained and chopped

1 lb. green beans

4 oz. shiitake mushrooms, sliced

2 tablespoons sesame oil

1 tablespoon soy sauce

2 tablespoons sesame seeds, for garnish

DIRECTIONS

1. To prepare the marinade, place all the ingredients in a small bowl and stir to combine.

2. To begin preparations for the casserole, place the marinade and the tofu in a resealable plastic bag, place it in the refrigerator, and let the tofu marinate for 2 days.

3. Preheat the oven to 375°F. Remove the cubes of tofu from the bag. Place the green beans, mushrooms, sesame oil, and soy sauce in the bag and shake until the vegetables are coated.

4. Line a 13 x 9–inch baking dish with parchment paper and place the tofu on it in an even layer. Place in the oven and roast for 35 minutes. Remove the pan from the oven, turn the cubes of tofu over, and push them to the edge of the pan. Add the green bean-and-mushroom mixture, return the pan to the oven, and roast for 15 minutes, or until the green beans are cooked to your preference. Remove the pan from the oven, garnish with the sesame seeds, and enjoy.

Yield: 4 Servings
Active Time: 10 Minutes
Total Time: 24 Hours

Ful Medames

INGREDIENTS

2 cups dried fava beans, soaked overnight and drained

4 garlic cloves, chopped

¼ cup extra-virgin olive oil, plus more to taste

Juice of 2 lemons

Salt and pepper, to taste

Large pinch of red pepper flakes

1 teaspoon cumin

2 hard-boiled eggs, each cut into 6 pieces

2 tablespoons finely chopped parsley or mint, for garnish

Feta cheese, crumbled, for serving (optional)

Black olives, for serving (optional)

DIRECTIONS

1. Place the fava beans in a Dutch oven, cover by ½ inch with water, and bring to a boil. Reduce the heat and simmer until tender, about 40 minutes. When the beans have about 10 minutes left to cook, stir in the garlic.

2. Drain, transfer the beans and garlic to a bowl, and add the olive oil, lemon juice, salt, pepper, red pepper flakes, and cumin. Stir to combine and lightly mash the beans with a fork.

3. Drizzle olive oil over the mixture, transfer it to a platter, and place the pieces of hard-boiled egg on top. Garnish with parsley or mint and, if desired, serve with the feta cheese and black olives.

Tofu Tacos

Yield: 4 Servings
Active Time: 15 Minutes
Total Time: 20 Minutes

INGREDIENTS

1 tablespoon extra-virgin olive oil, plus more as needed

1 lb. extra-firm tofu, drained and crumbled

1 tablespoon kosher salt

1 tablespoon cumin

1 tablespoon garlic powder

1 tablespoon cayenne powder

Adobo sauce, to taste

Corn Tortillas (see page 92), for serving

DIRECTIONS

1. Place the oil in a large skillet and warm over medium-high heat. Add the tofu, sprinkle the salt, cumin, garlic powder, and cayenne over the top, and stir until the tofu is coated. Cook until the tofu starts to brown, about 5 minutes.

2. Scramble the tofu and cook until it is browned all over, about 5 minutes.

3. Add the adobo sauce and more oil if the pan looks dry. Cook for 5 more minutes and then serve with the Corn Tortillas and your favorite taco fixings.

Yield: 4 Servings
Active Time: 20 Minutes
Total Time: 45 Minutes

Miso Ramen

INGREDIENTS

¼ cup sesame seeds

2 tablespoons sesame oil

4 garlic cloves, minced

2-inch piece of fresh ginger, peeled and minced

2 shallots, minced

2 teaspoons chili garlic sauce

6 tablespoons white miso paste

2 tablespoons sugar

2 tablespoons sake

8 cups Vegetable Stock (see page 119)

4 oz. ramen noodles

Salt and pepper, to taste

DIRECTIONS

1. Place the sesame seeds in a dry skillet and toast over medium heat until browned, about 2 minutes. Remove from the pan and use a mortar and pestle to grind them into a paste, adding water as needed.

2. Place the sesame oil in a large saucepan and warm over medium heat. When the oil starts to shimmer, add the garlic, ginger, and shallots and cook until fragrant, about 2 minutes.

3. Raise the heat to medium-high and add the chili garlic sauce, miso, toasted sesame paste, sugar, sake, and stock and stir to combine. Bring to a boil, reduce heat so that the soup simmers, and season with salt and pepper. Simmer for about 5 minutes and remove from heat.

4. While the soup is simmering, cook the noodles according to manufacturer's instructions. Drain the noodles and place them in warmed bowls. Pour the broth over the noodles and enjoy.

NOTE: If you're looking to add some substance to this ramen, top each portion with a poached egg.

Soba Noodles with Marinated Eggplant & Tofu

Yield: 4 Servings

Active Time: 45 Minutes

Total Time: 1 Hour and 45 Minutes

INGREDIENTS

For the Marinade

2 tablespoons rice vinegar

3 tablespoons soy sauce

1 tablespoon toasted sesame oil

½ teaspoon sugar

2 garlic cloves, minced

For the Dressing

1 tablespoon rice vinegar

1 tablespoon peanut oil

1 teaspoon soy sauce

1 tablespoon toasted sesame oil

1-inch piece of fresh ginger, peeled and grated

For the Noodles

2 small eggplants (about 2 lbs.)

8 oz. soba noodles

3 tablespoons peanut oil

Salt, to taste

12 oz. extra-firm tofu, drained and diced

6 scallions, trimmed and chopped, for garnish

DIRECTIONS

1. To prepare the marinade, place all of the ingredients in a small bowl and stir to combine. To prepare the dressing, place all of the ingredients in a separate small bowl and stir to combine. Set the marinade and the dressing aside.

2. To begin preparations for the noodles, trim both ends of the eggplants, slice them in half, and cut into ½-inch cubes. Place in a mixing bowl, add the marinade, and toss to combine. Let stand for 1 hour at room temperature.

3. Bring a large pot of water to a boil. Add the noodles and stir for the first minute to prevent any sticking. Cook until tender but still chewy, 5 to 7 minutes. Drain, rinse under cold water, drain again, and place in a large bowl. Add the dressing, toss to coat, and set aside.

4. Warm a wok or a large skillet over medium heat for 2 to 3 minutes. Raise heat to medium-high and add 2 tablespoons of the peanut oil. When it begins to shimmer, add the eggplant cubes and a couple pinches of salt and stir-fry until they soften and turn golden brown, 5 to 6 minutes. Using a slotted spoon, transfer the eggplant to a paper towel–lined plate. Add the remaining peanut oil and the tofu cubes to the pan and stir-fry until golden brown, 4 to 5 minutes. Using a slotted spoon, transfer the tofu to a separate paper towel–lined plate.

5. Divide the soba noodles between four bowls. Arrange the eggplant and tofu on top and garnish with the scallions.

Yield: 4 Servings
Active Time: 35 Minutes
Total Time: 1 Hour

Thai Fried Rice

INGREDIENTS

2 tablespoons extra-virgin olive oil, plus more as needed

8 oz. extra-firm tofu, drained and diced

3 tablespoons soy sauce

2 tablespoons rice vinegar

1 tablespoon sugar

1 shallot, diced

1 kohlrabi, peeled and diced

1-inch piece fresh ginger, peeled and minced

2 cups leftover rice

½ cup diced pineapple

¼ cup cashews

½ cup frozen peas

¼ cup finely chopped fresh cilantro, for garnish

Lime wedges, for serving

DIRECTIONS

1. Place 1 tablespoon of the oil in a large skillet and warm over high heat. When the oil starts to shimmer, add the tofu and sauté until it starts to brown, about 3 minutes.

2. Place the 2 tablespoons of the soy sauce, 1 tablespoon of the vinegar, and the sugar in a small bowl and stir to combine. Pour this mixture over the tofu and cook until the liquid has reduced to a glaze. Transfer the tofu to a bowl and set aside.

3. Add the shallot, kohlrabi, ginger and remaining oil to the pan. Sauté for 2 minutes and then add the rice. It is very likely that the rice will stick to the bottom of the pan. Do your best to scrape it off with a spatula. Cook the rice until it starts to brown, about 5 to 10 minutes, taking care not to let it become too mushy. Add the remaining soy sauce and rice vinegar and stir to incorporate.

4. Add the pineapple, cashews, frozen peas, and tofu to the pan. Gently fold to incorporate and cook for 2 minutes to heat everything through. Season to taste, garnish with the cilantro, and serve with lime wedges.

Buddha Seitan

INGREDIENTS

For the Sauce

½ cup water, plus more as needed

⅓ cup sugar

¼ cup mushroom soy sauce

½ cup soy sauce

¼ cup white wine vinegar

2 garlic cloves, minced

1-inch piece of fresh ginger, peeled and grated

For the Buddha Seitan

1 lb. seitan

⅓ cup canola oil, plus more as needed

⅓ cup cornstarch

8 oz. mushrooms, stemmed and quartered

1 shallot, minced .

8 oz. baby bok choy

Sesame seeds, for garnish

Jasmine rice, cooked, for serving

DIRECTIONS

1. To prepare the sauce, place all the ingredients in a bowl and whisk to combine. Set the sauce aside.

2. To begin preparations for the Buddha seitan, rinse the seitan to remove any broth and tear it into bite-sized pieces. Pat the seitan dry with paper towels. Place the canola oil in a small bowl and gradually add the cornstarch, stirring constantly to prevent lumps from forming.

3. Add canola oil to a Dutch oven until it is about 3 inches deep. Heat to 350°F or until a pea-sized bit of seitan dropped in the oil sizzles on contact. Dredge the pieces of seitan in the cornstarch mixture until completely coated. Working in batches, gently drop the seitan into the oil and fry, turning them so they cook evenly, for about 3 to 5 minutes. Transfer the cooked seitan to a paper towel–lined plate. Do not discard the cornstarch mixture because you will use it to thicken the sauce later.

4. Place a small amount of oil in a large skillet and warm it over medium heat. Add the mushrooms, making sure they are in one layer, and cook until they are browned all over, about 10 minutes. Transfer the mushrooms to a bowl, add the shallot to the pan, and sauté until it is fragrant, about 1 minute. Add the baby bok choy and cook until it starts to wilt, about 2 minutes. Transfer the mixture to the bowl containing the mushrooms.

5. Pour the sauce into the pan and scrape up any browned bits from the bottom of the pan. Bring to a boil, add a teaspoon of the cornstarch mixture, and stir until the sauce has thickened. If it does not thicken enough for your liking, add another teaspoon. If it is too thick, add a little water. When the sauce has reached the desired consistency, return the seitan and vegetables to the pan and toss to coat. Sprinkle the sesame seeds on top and serve over the rice.

Saag Aloo

Yield: 4 Servings
Active Time: 15 Minutes
Total Time: 30 Minutes

INGREDIENTS

1 tablespoon extra-virgin olive oil

8 oz. fingerling or Red Bliss potatoes, chopped

1 small onion, chopped

1 teaspoon mustard seeds

1 teaspoon cumin

1 garlic clove, chopped

1-inch piece of fresh ginger, peeled and grated

1 lb. frozen spinach

1 teaspoon red pepper flakes

½ cup water

Salt, to taste

2 tablespoons plain yogurt, or to taste

DIRECTIONS

1. Place the oil and potatoes in a Dutch oven or a large skillet and cook over medium heat until the potatoes just start to brown, about 5 minutes.

2. Add the onion, mustard seeds, and cumin and cook until the onion starts to soften, about 5 minutes. Add the garlic and ginger and cook, stirring constantly, until fragrant, about 2 minutes.

3. Add the frozen spinach, the red pepper flakes, and water and cover the Dutch oven or skillet with a lid. Cook, stirring occasionally, until the spinach is heated through, about 10 minutes.

4. Remove the cover and cook until all of the liquid has evaporated. Season with salt, add the yogurt, and stir to incorporate. Add more yogurt if you prefer a creamier dish, stir to incorporate, and serve.

Yield: 4 Servings
Active Time: 30 Minutes
Total Time: 1 Hour

Tofu San Bei

INGREDIENTS

3 tablespoons peanut oil

1 lb. extra-firm tofu, drained and chopped

1½ teaspoons cornstarch, plus more as needed

3 tablespoons toasted sesame oil

8 garlic cloves, smashed

2-inch piece fresh ginger, peeled and chopped into 8 pieces

10 scallions, trimmed and chopped

Salt, to taste

3 tablespoons sugar

¾ cup water, plus 1 tablespoon

¾ cup Shaoxing rice wine

⅓ cup soy sauce

6 oz. ramen noodles

2 handfuls of fresh Thai basil leaves, sliced thin, for garnish

DIRECTIONS

1. Warm a large skillet over medium heat for 3 minutes. Add the peanut or grapeseed oil and warm until it starts to shimmer. Dredge the tofu slices in a shallow dish containing cornstarch and tap to remove any excess. Working in batches, add the tofu to the skillet in a single layer. Raise the heat to medium-high and cook until the tofu is browned all over, 3 to 4 minutes per side. Transfer to a paper towel–lined plate to drain.

2. Wipe out the skillet and add the sesame oil to the pan. Reduce heat to medium and add the smashed garlic, ginger, scallions, and two pinches of salt once the oil starts to shimmer. Cook, stirring frequently, until fragrant, about 2 minutes. Add the sugar and stir until it has melted. Stir in the ¾ cup water, rice wine, and soy sauce, raise heat to medium-high, and bring to a boil. Reduce the heat to low, cover, and simmer, stirring occasionally, for 10 minutes.

3. Place the 1½ teaspoons cornstarch and 1 tablespoon water in a small bowl and stir to combine. Add the mixture to the sauce and stir until thoroughly incorporated. Continue to cook, stirring occasionally, until the sauce thickens slightly, about 5 minutes. Add the tofu slices and cook until warmed through, about 3 minutes.

4. As the sauce simmers, bring a large pot of water to a boil. Add the ramen noodles and stir for the first minute to prevent any sticking. Cook until tender and chewy, drain, and divide the noodles between four warm, shallow bowls. Top with the tofu slices, ladle the sauce over the top, garnish with the basil, and serve.

Polenta with Corn, Peppers & Tomatillos

Yield: 4 Servings
Active Time: 40 Minutes
Total Time: 1 Hour

INGREDIENTS

1 tablespoon extra-virgin olive oil, plus more as needed

1 onion, diced

1 cup corn kernels

½ bell pepper, stems and seeds removed, chopped

1 small jalapeño chile pepper, stems and seeds removed, chopped (optional)

½ lb. tomatillos, husked, rinsed, and chopped

1 teaspoon cumin

1½ teaspoons kosher salt

1 garlic clove, minced

1 cup milk

2 cups water, plus more as needed

1 cup medium-grain polenta

2 tablespoons unsalted butter

1 cup grated cheddar cheese, plus more for garnish

¼ cup chopped fresh cilantro, for garnish

DIRECTIONS

1. Place the oil in a large skillet and warm it over medium-high heat. Add the onion and sauté until it starts to brown, about 5 minutes. Add the corn and continue to cook, adding more oil if the pan becomes too dry. When the corn starts to brown, add the pepper, jalapeño (if using), tomatillos, cumin, and 1 teaspoon of the salt. Cook until the tomatillos start to collapse, about 5 minutes. Add the garlic and cook until fragrant, about 2 minutes. Remove the pan from heat and set it aside.

2. Place the milk, water, and remaining salt in a medium saucepan and bring it to a boil. Add the polenta slowly, while stirring constantly to prevent lumps from forming. Reduce the heat to a simmer and cook for 2 minutes, stirring continuously. Cover the pan and cook for about 40 minutes, until the polenta is thick and creamy, stirring every 10 minutes. If the polenta absorbs all of the liquid before it is cooked, add up to 1 cup water.

3. Stir the butter and cheese into the polenta. To serve, ladle the polenta onto a plate and top with a large spoonful of the corn-and-tomatillo mixture. Garnish with the cilantro and additional cheddar cheese.

Yield: 4 Servings
Active Time: 20 Minutes
Total Time: 30 Minutes

Green Shakshuka

INGREDIENTS

1 tablespoon extra-virgin olive oil

1 onion, chopped

2 garlic cloves, minced

½ lb. tomatillos, husked, rinsed, and chopped

1 (12 oz.) package of frozen spinach

1 teaspoon coriander

¼ cup water

Salt and pepper, to taste

4 eggs

Tabasco, for serving (optional)

DIRECTIONS

1. Place the oil in a large skillet and warm it over medium-high heat. Add the onion and cook, stirring frequently, until it just starts to soften, about 5 minutes. Add the garlic and cook until fragrant, about 2 minutes. Add the tomatillos and cook until they start to collapse, about 5 minutes.

2. Add the spinach, coriander, and water and cook, breaking up the spinach with a wooden spoon, until the spinach is completely thawed and blended with the tomatillos. Season with salt and pepper.

3. Evenly spread the mixture in the pan and then make four indentations in the mixture. Crack an egg into each indentation. Reduce the heat to medium, cover the pan, and let the eggs cook until the whites are set, 3 to 5 minutes. Serve with Tabasco, if desired.

Sweet Potato Gnocchi

Yield: 4 Servings
Active Time: 1 Hour
Total Time: 2 Hours and 30 Minutes

INGREDIENTS

2½ lbs. sweet potatoes

½ cup ricotta cheese

1 egg

2 egg yolks

1 tablespoon kosher salt, plus more to taste

1 teaspoon black pepper

3 tablespoons light brown sugar

2 tablespoons real maple syrup

2 cups all-purpose flour, plus more as needed

1 cup semolina flour

2 tablespoons extra-virgin olive oil

Parmesan cheese, freshly grated, for garnish

DIRECTIONS

1. Preheat the oven to 350°F. Wash the sweet potatoes, place them on a parchment-lined baking sheet, and use a knife to pierce several holes in the potatoes. Place in the oven and roast until they are soft all the way through, 45 minutes to 1 hour. Remove from the oven, slice them open, and let cool completely.

2. Scrape the cooled sweet potato flesh into a mixing bowl and mash until smooth. Add the ricotta, egg, egg yolks, salt, pepper, brown sugar, and maple syrup and stir until thoroughly combined. Add the flours 1 cup at a time and work the mixture with your hands until incorporated. The dough should not feel tacky when touched. If it is tacky, incorporate more all-purpose flour, 1 teaspoon at a time, until it has the right texture. Coat a mixing bowl with the olive oil and set it aside.

3. Transfer the dough to a lightly floured work surface and cut it into 10 even pieces. Roll each piece into a long rope and cut the ropes into ¾-inch-wide pieces. Roll the gnocchi over a fork, or a gnocchi board, pressing down gently to form them into the desired shapes. Place the formed gnocchi on a parchment-lined, flour-dusted baking sheet.

4. To cook the gnocchi, bring a large pot of water to a boil. Add salt once the water is boiling. Working in small batches, add the gnocchi and stir to keep them from sticking to the bottom. The gnocchi will eventually float to the surface. Cook for 1 more minute, remove, and transfer to the bowl containing the olive oil. Toss to coat, place in a skillet, and brown the gnocchi on both sides. Garnish with Parmesan and enjoy.

No-Knead Pizza Dough

Yield: 4 Balls of Dough
Active Time: 10 Minutes
Total Time: 22 Hours

INGREDIENTS

16.2 oz. water

⅛ teaspoon plus 1 pinch active dry yeast

22.6 oz. bread flour

1 tablespoon table salt

DIRECTIONS

1. Warm 3½ tablespoons of the water until it is about 105°F. Add the water and the yeast to a bowl and gently stir. Let the mixture sit until it starts to foam.

2. In a large bowl, combine the flour, salt, yeast mixture, and remaining water. Work the mixture until there are no more lumps remaining in the dough. Cover the bowl with plastic wrap and let the mixture rest until it has doubled in size, 16 to 20 hours.

3. Divide the dough into four pieces and shape them into tight rounds. Cover with a damp kitchen towel and let them rest for 2 hours before making pizza.

Squash Blossom & Ricotta Pizza

Yield: 1 Pizza
Active Time: 15 Minutes
Total Time: 45 Minutes

INGREDIENTS

Semolina flour, as needed

1 ball of pizza dough (see page 186 for homemade)

Extra-virgin olive oil, to taste

4 oz. low-moisture mozzarella cheese, shredded

3 squash blossoms, stamens removed, sliced lengthwise

3 oz. ricotta cheese

Salt and pepper, to taste

Zest of 1 lemon

DIRECTIONS

1. Preheat the oven to the maximum temperature and place a baking stone or steel on the bottom of the oven as it warms. Dust a work surface with semolina flour, place the dough on the surface, and gently stretch it into a round.

2. Drizzle olive oil over the dough, cover with the shredded mozzarella, and distribute the squash blossoms over the cheese. You want to open the squash blossoms up so that they cover as much of the pizza as possible. Distribute dollops of the ricotta over the pizza, season with salt and pepper, and drizzle more olive oil over the top.

3. Dust a peel or a flat baking sheet with semolina and use it to transfer the pizza to the heated baking implement in the oven. Bake for 15 minutes, until the crust is golden brown and starting to char. Remove, sprinkle the lemon zest over the pizza, and let it cool slightly before serving.

Artichoke & Potato Pizza

Yield: 1 Pizza

Active Time: 20 Minutes

Total Time: 1 Hour

INGREDIENTS

Salt and pepper, to taste

1 potato, peeled and sliced thin

Semolina flour, as needed

1 ball of pizza dough (see page 186 for homemade)

Extra-virgin olive oil, to taste

3 oz. low-moisture mozzarella cheese, shredded

4 artichoke hearts in olive oil, drained and chopped

Fresh rosemary, to taste

DIRECTIONS

1. Preheat the oven to the maximum temperature and place a baking stone or steel on the bottom of the oven as it warms. Bring a pot of salted water to a boil and prepare an ice water bath. Add the potato to the boiling water and cook until it is translucent, 2 to 4 minutes. Drain, transfer the potato to the ice water bath, and let sit for 2 minutes. Drain again and pat dry.

2. Dust a work surface with the semolina flour, place the dough on the surface, and gently stretch it into a round. Drizzle olive oil over the dough, cover with the shredded mozzarella, and distribute the potato and artichoke over the cheese. Season with salt and pepper, drizzle olive oil over the pizza, and sprinkle a generous amount of rosemary on top.

3. Dust a peel or a flat baking sheet with semolina and use it to transfer the pizza to the heated baking implement in the oven. Bake for about 15 minutes, until the crust is golden brown and starting to char. Remove and let the pizza cool slightly before slicing and serving.

Yield: 1 Pizza
Active Time: 30 Minutes
Total Time: 1 Hour and 15 Minutes

Ortolana

INGREDIENTS

¼ cup mushrooms, chopped

Salt and pepper, to taste

Extra-virgin olive oil, to taste

½ bell pepper, sliced

½ small eggplant, sliced

Semolina flour, as needed

1 ball of pizza dough (see page 186 for homemade)

⅓ cup Perfect Pizza Sauce (see page 46)

¼ onion, sliced

Fresh basil leaves, to taste

Dried oregano, to taste

DIRECTIONS

1. Preheat the oven to the maximum temperature and place a baking stone or steel on the bottom of the oven as it warms. Place the mushrooms in a bowl, season with salt and pepper, and generously drizzle olive oil over them. Stir to combine and let the mixture sit for 10 minutes. Drain and set aside.

2. Place the bell pepper and eggplant on an aluminum foil–lined baking sheet, season with salt and pepper, drizzle olive oil over the vegetables, and place in the oven. Roast until they are tender and browned, about 25 minutes. Remove from the oven and let cool.

3. Dust a work surface with the semolina flour, place the dough on the surface, and gently stretch it into a round. Cover the dough with the sauce and top with the mushrooms, eggplant, peppers, onion, and basil leaves.

4. Season the pizza with salt and drizzle olive oil over the top.

5. Dust a peel or a flat baking sheet with semolina and use it to transfer the pizza to the heated baking implement in the oven. Bake for about 15 minutes, until the crust is golden brown and starting to char. Remove and let cool slightly before slicing and serving.

Mushroom Barbacoa

Yield: 4 Servings
Active Time: 1 hour
Total Time: 8 hours

INGREDIENTS

1 tablespoon coriander seeds

½ teaspoon whole cloves

½ teaspoon allspice berries

½ teaspoon cumin seeds

1½ tablespoons black peppercorns

1 ancho chile pepper, stems and seeds removed

1 guajillo chile pepper, stems and seeds removed

1 chipotle chile pepper, stems and seeds removed

1 pasilla chile pepper, stems and seeds removed

1 cup orange juice

1 cup fresh lime juice

Salt, to taste

2¼ lbs. mushrooms (shiitake, cremini, and/or oyster), julienned

2 small onions, sliced, plus more for serving

5 garlic cloves

2 bay leaves

2 avocado leaves (optional)

Banana leaves, spines removed and toasted, as needed

Corn Tortillas (see page 92), for serving

Salsa Verde (see page 53), for serving

Fresh cilantro, chopped, for serving

Lime wedges, for serving

DIRECTIONS

1. Place the coriander, cloves, allspice, cumin, and peppercorns in a dry skillet and toast until fragrant, shaking the pan frequently. Use a mortar and pestle or a spice grinder to grind the mixture into a powder.

2. Place the chiles in the skillet and toast until they are fragrant and pliable. Transfer the chiles to a bowl of hot water and soak for 20 minutes.

3. Drain the chiles and reserve the soaking liquid. Place the chiles, one of the onions, garlic, and some of the soaking liquid in a blender and puree until smooth. Add the toasted spice powder, orange and lime juice, and pulse until incorporated.

4. Season the mixture with salt and place it in a mixing bowl. Add the mushrooms and let them marinate for at least 6 hours.

5. Preheat the oven to 420°F. Remove the mushrooms from the marinade and place them in the banana leaves. Layer the onions, garlic, bay leaves, and avocado leaves (if using) on top, fold the banana leaves over to form a packet, and tie it closed with kitchen twine.

6. Place the packet on a parchment-lined baking sheet, place it in the oven, and roast for 20 minutes.

7. Remove from the oven and open the packet. Return to the oven and roast for an additional 10 to 15 minutes to caramelize the mushrooms.

8. Remove from the oven and serve with tortillas, Salsa Verde, additional onion, cilantro, and lime wedges.

Mushroom Barbacoa, see page 193

Orecchiette with Greens & Potatoes

Yield: 4 Servings
Active Time: 20 Minutes
Total Time: 30 Minutes

INGREDIENTS

6 tablespoons extra-virgin olive oil, plus 1 teaspoon

2 garlic cloves, halved

1 teaspoon capers, drained, rinsed, and minced

½ cup green olives, pitted and minced

2 large russet potatoes, peeled and chopped

⅛ teaspoon cayenne pepper

Salt and black pepper, to taste

12 oz. orecchiette

8 oz. arugula or baby spinach

¼ cup grated Pecorino Romano cheese, plus more for garnish

DIRECTIONS

1. Place 6 tablespoons of the olive oil in a large, deep skillet and warm it over low heat. Add the garlic, capers, olives, and cayenne and sauté until the garlic starts to brown, about 3 minutes. Discard the garlic and remove the pan from heat.

2. Bring salted water to a boil in a large saucepan. Add the potatoes. When the water returns to a boil, add the pasta and cook according to manufacturer's instructions. Add the greens 1 minute prior to draining the pasta. Reserve ½ cup of the pasta water, drain, and return the pot to the stove.

3. Set the skillet containing the sauce over medium-high heat. Add reserved pasta water to the pot, turn heat to high and add the pasta, potatoes, greens, and the remaining olive oil. Toss until the water has been absorbed. Transfer the mixture to the skillet and cook, tossing to combine, for 2 minutes. Add the Pecorino and toss until distributed. Season the dish with salt and pepper and garnish with additional Pecorino before serving.

Butternut Squash Ravioli

Yield: 4 Servings

Active Time: 30 Minutes

Total Time: 1 Hour and 30 Minutes

INGREDIENTS

For the Filling

1½ lbs. butternut squash, halved lengthwise and seeded

Extra-virgin olive oil, as needed

¼ cup fresh bread crumbs

½ cup freshly grated Parmesan cheese, plus more for garnish

¼ cup crumbled gorgonzola cheese

2 egg yolks, beaten

1 teaspoon freshly grated nutmeg

10 fresh rosemary leaves, finely chopped

Salt, to taste

For the Dough

2 cups "00" flour, plus more as needed

Pinch of kosher salt

9 egg yolks, beaten

2 teaspoons extra-virgin olive oil

1 egg

1 tablespoon water

DIRECTIONS

1. Preheat the oven to 375°F. To prepare the filling, brush the flesh of the squash with olive oil and place them, cut side up, on parchment-lined baking sheets. Place the squash in the oven and roast until fork-tender, 40 to 45 minutes. Remove from the oven and let cool, then scoop the flesh into a bowl and mash until smooth. Add the bread crumbs, cheeses, egg yolks, nutmeg, and rosemary to the squash and stir until thoroughly combined. Season the filling with salt and set it aside.

2. To begin preparations for the dough, place the flour and salt in a mixing bowl, stir to combine, and make a well in the center. Place the egg yolks and olive oil in the well and slowly incorporate the flour until the dough holds together. Knead the dough until smooth, about 5 minutes. Cover the bowl with plastic wrap and let stand at room temperature for 30 minutes.

3. To form the ravioli, divide the dough into two pieces. Use a pasta maker to roll each piece into a long, thin rectangle. Place one of the rectangles over a flour-dusted ravioli tray and place a teaspoon of the butternut filling into each of the depressions. Place the egg and water in a small bowl and beat until combined. Dip a pastry brush or a finger into the egg wash and lightly coat the edge of each ravioli with it. Gently lay the other rectangle over the piece in the ravioli tray. Use a rolling pin to gently cut out the ravioli. Remove the cut ravioli and place them on a flour-dusted baking sheet.

4. Bring a large saucepan of salted water to a boil. When the water is boiling, add the ravioli, stir to make sure they do not stick to the bottom, and cook until tender but still chewy, about 2 minutes.

5. Drain, divide the ravioli between the serving plates, and garnish with additional Parmesan.

Yield: 6 Servings

Active Time: 35 Minutes

Total Time: 1 Hour

Rotolo

INGREDIENTS

5 tablespoons extra-virgin olive oil, plus more as needed

10 scallions, trimmed and sliced thin

Salt, to taste

1 lb. cremini mushrooms, stemmed and minced

1 lb. extra-firm tofu, drained and cut into ½-inch slices

4 cups shredded cabbage

4 carrots, peeled and grated

3 tablespoons water

2 tablespoons sugar

1 teaspoon white pepper

4 teaspoons cornstarch

6 flat lasagna sheets

2 handfuls of fresh parsley, chopped, plus more for garnish

2 cups Marinara Sauce (see page 42), warmed

DIRECTIONS

1. Place the olive oil in a large skillet and warm it over medium heat. When it begins to shimmer, add the scallions and a pinch of salt and sauté until the scallions are translucent, about 3 minutes. Raise the heat to medium-high, add the mushrooms, tofu, cabbage, and carrots and sauté until all the vegetables start to soften, about 5 minutes.

2. Place 2 tablespoons of the water, the sugar, and pepper in a small bowl. Place the cornstarch and the remaining water in another bowl, whisk it until smooth, and then whisk it into the water-and-sugar mixture. Stir the resulting mixture into the skillet and raise the heat to high. Cook until the liquid has evaporated and the vegetables are cooked through, about 2 minutes. Remove the pan from heat and let the mixture cool slightly. Transfer it to a food processor and pulse until it is a chunky puree. Season with salt and set it aside.

3. Bring a large pot of water to a boil. Once it's boiling, add salt and a single lasagna sheet. Cook for 1 minute, retrieve the sheet using two large slotted spoons, transfer to a kitchen towel, and let it cool. Repeat until all the lasagna sheets have been cooked.

4. Preheat the oven to 475°F. Generously grease a 15 x 10-inch baking pan with olive oil. Working with one sheet at a time, lay it on a work surface covered with parchment paper. Using a rubber spatula, spread some of the puree over the sheet and sprinkle some of the parsley on top. Starting at one short end, roll the sheet up tightly. Once you are done rolling, rest it on its seam to keep it from unrolling, or secure the roll with toothpicks. When all of the sheets and filling have been used up, slice each roll into 1¼-inch-thick rounds. Place them in the baking dish, making sure to leave space between. Place the pan in the oven and bake until lightly browned on top and heated through, 10 to 12 minutes.

5. To serve, place 2 to 3 tablespoons of the sauce on a warm plate, arrange three rotolo on top, and garnish with additional parsley.

Eggplant Parmesan

Yield: 4 Servings
Active Time: 20 Minutes
Total Time: 1 Hour

INGREDIENTS

1 large eggplant
(about 1½ lbs.)

Salt, to taste

2 tablespoons extra-virgin
olive oil

1 cup Italian bread crumbs

¼ cup freshly grated
Parmesan cheese

1 egg, beaten

Marinara Sauce (see page
42), as needed

2 garlic cloves, minced

8 oz. shredded mozzarella
cheese

Fresh basil, finely chopped,
for garnish

DIRECTIONS

1. Preheat the oven to 350°F. Trim the top and bottom off the eggplant and slice it into ¼-inch-thick slices. Put the slices on paper towels in a single layer, sprinkle salt over them, and let rest for about 15 minutes. Turn the slices over, salt the other side, and let them rest for another 15 minutes. Rinse the eggplant and pat dry with paper towels.

2. Drizzle the oil over a baking sheet. In a shallow bowl, combine the bread crumbs and Parmesan cheese. Put the beaten egg in another shallow bowl. Dip the slices of eggplant in the egg and then in the bread crumb-and-cheese mixture until both sides are coated. Place the breaded slices on the baking sheet.

3. When all of the eggplant has been breaded, place it in the oven and bake for 10 minutes. Remove, turn the slices over, and bake for another 10 minutes. Remove the eggplant from the oven and let it cool slightly.

4. Place a layer of sauce in a square baking dish or a cast-iron skillet and stir in the garlic. Lay some of the eggplant slices on top of the sauce, top them with more sauce, and then arrange the remaining eggplant on top. Sprinkle the mozzarella over the eggplant.

5. Place the dish in the oven and bake for about 30 minutes, until the sauce is bubbling and the cheese is golden brown. Remove from the oven and let cool for 10 minutes before serving with additional Marinara Sauce and fresh basil.

Porcini Mushroom & Béchamel Lasagna

Yield: 6 Servings
Active Time: 1 Hour
Total Time: 2 Hours

INGREDIENTS

1 cup dry red wine

2 tablespoons unsalted butter

3 shallots, minced

Salt and pepper, to taste

2 garlic cloves, peeled and minced

1 lb. cremini mushrooms, stemmed and sliced thin

1 oz. dried porcini mushrooms, reconstituted and chopped, soaking liquid reserved

Béchamel Sauce (see sidebar)

12 oz. dried lasagna noodles

2 tablespoons finely chopped fresh thyme, plus more for garnish

1½ cups freshly grated Parmesan cheese

DIRECTIONS

1. Place the wine in a small saucepan and bring it to a boil. Cook until it has reduced almost by half, about 5 minutes. Remove the pan from heat and set it aside.

2. Place the butter in a large, deep skillet and melt it over medium heat. Add the shallots and a pinch of salt and sauté until the shallots are translucent, about 3 minutes. Reduce the temperature to low, cover the pan, and cook, stirring occasionally, until the shallots have softened, about 10 minutes. Stir in the garlic and sauté for 30 seconds.

3. Raise the heat to medium-high, add the cremini and porcini mushrooms and the thyme, season with salt, and cook, while stirring frequently, until the mushrooms begin to release their liquid, about 5 minutes. Add the reduced wine, the porcini soaking liquid, and bring to a gentle simmer. Cook, stirring occasionally, until the mushrooms are tender and the liquid has reduced by half, 12 to 15 minutes. Remove from the heat, season to taste, and then stir in the Béchamel Sauce.

4. Cover the bottom of a deep 13 x 9-inch baking dish with some of the mushroom mixture. Cover with a layer of noodles, making sure they are slightly overlapping. Cover with a layer of the mushroom mixture and sprinkle ½ cup of the Parmesan on top. Repeat this layering two more times, concluding with a layer of the mushroom mixture topped with the remaining Parmesan.

5. Cover the pan loosely with aluminum foil, place it in the oven, and bake for 35 minutes. Remove the foil and continue to bake until the edges of the lasagna sheets are lightly browned, about 12 minutes. For nice, clean slices, remove the lasagna from the oven and allow it to rest for at least 20 minutes before slicing.

Bechamel Sauce

Place 1 stick of unsalted butter in a medium saucepan and melt it over medium heat. Add ½ cup flour and cook, stirring constantly, for 5 minutes, until the mixture stops foaming and turns golden brown. Add ½ cup of whole milk and stir vigorously until you've loosened the mixture. Incorporate another 3½ cups milk and cook, stirring constantly, until the mixture starts to thicken. Stir in ½ teaspoon freshly grated nutmeg and season with salt and pepper.

Autumn Risotto

Yield: 6 Servings

Active Time: 35 Minutes

Total Time: 1 Hour and 20 Minutes

INGREDIENTS

4 oz. unsalted butter

2 yellow onions, chopped

1 small butternut squash, peeled, seeds removed, and chopped

1 tablespoon kosher salt, plus 2 teaspoons

3 cups whole milk

5 cups Vegetable Stock (see page 119)

2 cups Arborio rice

2 cups white wine

3 cups baby kale, chopped

¾ cup toasted walnuts

½ cup dried cranberries

Fresh lemon juice, to taste

DIRECTIONS

1. Place 2 tablespoons of the butter in a saucepan and melt it over medium heat. Add one of the onions and cook until it is translucent, about 3 minutes. Add the squash, the tablespoon of salt, and the milk, reduce the heat to low, and cook until the squash is tender, about 20 minutes. Strain, discard the cooking liquid, and transfer the squash and onion to a blender. Puree until smooth and then set aside.

2. Place the stock in a saucepan, bring to a boil, and remove from heat.

3. Place the remaining butter in a large skillet with high sides and melt over medium heat. Add the remaining onion and sauté until translucent, about 3 minutes. Add the rice and remaining salt and cook, stirring constantly, until you can smell a toasted nutty aroma. Be careful not to brown the rice.

4. Deglaze the pan with the white wine and continue to stir until all the liquid has been absorbed. Add the stock in 1-cup increments and stir constantly until all the stock has been absorbed by the rice.

5. Add the squash puree and kale, stir to incorporate, and season to taste. Stir in the walnuts, dried cranberries, and lemon juice, and serve immediately.

Chiles Relleno

INGREDIENTS

6 large poblano chile
peppers

1 lb. Oaxaca or Monterey
Jack cheese

4 egg whites

4 egg yolks

2 cups all-purpose flour

2 cups canola oil

2 large tomatoes

2 garlic cloves

¼ white onion

Salt, to taste

1 teaspoon dried Mexican
oregano

DIRECTIONS

1. Roast the poblanos over an open flame, on the grill, or in the oven until charred all over. Place them in a bowl, cover it with plastic wrap, and let them sit for 5 minutes.

2. Remove the chiles from the bowl and remove the charred skin with your hands.

3. Using a sharp paring knife, make a cut close to the stems of the peppers. Remove the seed pod, but leave the stems attached.

4. Stuff the chiles with 1 to 2 ounces of cheese (the amount depends on the size of the chile) and use toothpicks to seal the small cuts you've made.

5. In the work bowl of a stand mixer fitted with the whisk attachment, add the egg whites and whip on high until they hold stiff peaks.

6. Add the egg yolks, reduce the speed to low, and beat until just incorporated, about 30 seconds. Add ½ cup of flour and again beat until just incorporated, as you do not want to overwork the batter.

7. Place the oil in a large, deep skillet and warm it to 325°F.

8. Bring water to a boil in a medium saucepan. Add the tomatoes, garlic, and onion and cook until tender, about 7 minutes. Drain, place the vegetables in a blender, and puree until smooth. Season the sauce with salt, stir in the oregano, and set it aside.

9. Place the remaining flour on a baking sheet. Dip the chiles into the flour until coated on all sides. Dip the chiles into the batter and gently slip them into the oil.

10. Fry the chiles until crispy and golden brown, about 5 minutes, making sure you turn them just once. Drain on a paper towel–lined plate.

11. When all of the chiles have been cooked, serve them alongside the tomato sauce.

Chilaquiles

Yield: 4 Servings
Active time: 30 Minutes
Total time: 35 Minutes

INGREDIENTS

4 large tomatoes

2 garlic cloves

½ white onion, sliced thin

2 guajillo chile peppers, stemmed and seeded

2 dried chiles de arbol, stemmed and seeded

2 cups canola oil

1 lb. Corn Tortillas (see page 92), cut into triangles

Salt, to taste

4 large eggs

2 cups shredded queso fresco

DIRECTIONS

1. Bring water to a boil in a medium saucepan. Add the tomatoes, garlic, and half of the onion and cook until tender, about 7 minutes.

2. Place the chiles in a bowl and pour some of the hot water over them. Let the chiles soak for 15 minutes.

3. Drain the remaining water, place the vegetables in a blender, and puree until smooth. Leave the puree in the blender.

4. Place the canola oil in a deep skillet and warm it to 350°F. Add the tortillas and fry until crispy, about 3 minutes. Place the fried tortillas on a paper towel–lined plate and let them drain.

5. Preheat the oven to 350°F. Add the chiles to the puree in the blender and blitz until smooth. Season the puree generously with salt and set it aside.

6. Place the olive oil in a large cast-iron skillet and warm over medium heat. Add the remaining onion and cook until translucent, about 3 minutes.

7. Add the sauce and the tortillas to the skillet and stir until everything is coated in the sauce. Crack the eggs on top, crumble the queso fresco over everything, and place the skillet in the oven.

8. Bake until the egg whites are set and the cheese is slightly melted. Serve with additional cheese and cilantro.

Yield: 16 Samosa

Active Time: 45 Minutes

Total Time: 1 Hour and
30 Minutes

Punjabi Samosa

INGREDIENTS

For the Wrappers

2 cups maida flour, plus
more as needed

¼ teaspoon kosher salt

2 tablespoons extra-virgin
olive oil

½ cup water, plus more
as needed

For the Filling

2 russet potatoes, peeled
and chopped

2 tablespoons extra-virgin
olive oil

1 teaspoon coriander seeds,
crushed

½ teaspoon fennel seeds,
crushed

Pinch of fenugreek seeds,
crushed

1-inch piece of fresh ginger,
peeled and grated

1 garlic clove, grated

1 teaspoon minced jalapeño
chile pepper

2 teaspoons chili powder

¾ teaspoon turmeric

1 tablespoon amchoor
powder

½ teaspoon garam masala

Salt, to taste

Canola oil, as needed

DIRECTIONS

1. To begin preparations for the wrappers, place the flour and salt in a mixing bowl and use your hands to combine. Add the oil and work the mixture with your hands until it is a coarse meal. Add the water and knead the mixture until it comes together as a smooth, firm dough. If the dough is too dry, incorporate more water, adding 1 tablespoon at a time. Cover the bowl with a kitchen towel and set aside.

2. To begin preparations for the filling, place the potatoes in a saucepan and cover with water. Bring the water to a boil and cook until fork-tender, about 20 minutes. Transfer to a bowl, mash until smooth, and set aside.

3. Place the olive oil in a skillet and warm over medium heat. Add the crushed seeds and toast until fragrant, about 2 minutes, shaking the pan frequently. Add the ginger, garlic, and jalapeño, stir-fry for 2 minutes, and then add the chili powder, turmeric, amchoor powder, and garam masala. Cook for another minute before adding the mashed potatoes. Stir to combine, season with salt, and taste the mixture. Adjust the seasoning as necessary, transfer the mixture to a bowl, and let it cool completely.

4. Divide the dough for the wrappers into eight pieces and roll each one out into a 6-inch circle on a flour-dusted work surface. Cut the circles in half and brush the flat edge of each piece with water. Fold one corner of the flat edge toward the other to make a cone and pinch to seal. Fill each cone one-third of the way with the filling, brush the opening with water, and pinch to seal. Place the sealed samosas on a parchment-lined baking sheet.

5. Add canola oil to a Dutch oven until it is 2 inches deep and warm to 325°F over medium heat. Working in batches, add the filled samosas to the hot oil and fry, turning them as they cook, until they are golden brown, about 5 minutes. Transfer the cooked samosas to a paper towel–lined plate and serve once they have all been cooked.

Desserts

When the time comes to make something special for the all-important last course, there's no reason to take the ball out of Mother Nature's hands, as her ability to effortlessly infuse products with sweetness and tartness is the envy of the culinary world. In fact, her facility is such that it's simply criminal not to celebrate it.

CRIMPING A PIECRUST

Crimping creates a decorative edge on your piecrust. It also defines it, keeping it from folding over in the oven. To crimp a piecrust, place your left thumb and left index finger approximately 1 inch from each other. Crook your right index finger and work your way around the pie plate, pressing your right index finger into that 1-inch space and against the inside edge of the piecrust.

Yield: 2 (9-Inch) Piecrusts

Active Time: 15 Minutes

Total Time: 2 Hours and 15 Minutes

Perfect Piecrusts

INGREDIENTS

8 oz. unsalted butter, cubed

12.5 oz. all-purpose flour, plus more as needed

½ teaspoon kosher salt

4 teaspoons sugar

½ cup ice water

DIRECTIONS

1. Place the butter in a small bowl and place it in the freezer.

2. Place the flour, salt, and sugar in a food processor and pulse a few times until combined.

3. Add the chilled butter and pulse until the mixture is crumbly, consisting of pea-sized clumps.

4. Add the water and pulse until the mixture comes together as a dough.

5. Place the dough on a flour-dusted work surface and fold it over itself until it is a ball. Divide the dough in two and flatten each piece into a 1-inch-thick disk. Cover each piece in plastic wrap and place in the refrigerator for at least 2 hours before rolling out to fit your pie plate.

Coconut Pudding Pancakes

Yield: 30 Pancakes

Active Time: 20 Minutes

Total Time: 50 Minutes

INGREDIENTS

1½ cups coconut milk

1½ cups rice flour

½ cup sweetened shredded coconut

5 tablespoons caster sugar

½ teaspoon fine sea salt

1 cup coconut cream

½ tablespoon tapioca starch or cornstarch

2 tablespoons canola oil

¼ cup corn kernels (optional)

DIRECTIONS

1. Preheat the oven to 350°F and coat an aebleskiver pan with nonstick cooking spray.

2. Place the coconut milk, 1 cup of the rice flour, the coconut, 1 tablespoon of the sugar, and the salt in a bowl and whisk vigorously until the sugar has dissolved. Set the mixture aside.

3. Place the coconut cream, remaining rice flour, remaining sugar, and tapioca starch or cornstarch in another bowl and whisk until the starch has dissolved. Add this mixture to the coconut milk mixture and stir until combined.

4. Fill the wells of the aebleskiver pan with the batter and top with some of the corn, if using.

5. Place the pan in the oven and bake until they are firm, 15 to 20 minutes. Remove from the oven, transfer the cooked cakes to a platter, and tent it with aluminum foil to keep warm. Repeat Steps 4 and 5 with any remaining batter.

Beet Panna Cotta

Yield: 4 Servings

Active Time: 30 Minutes

Total Time: 4 Hours and 30 Minutes

INGREDIENTS

4 sheets of silver gelatin

13 oz. heavy cream

9 oz. milk

4 oz. sugar

1.8 oz. honey

12 oz. red beets, peeled and finely diced

4 oz. goat cheese, crumbled

DIRECTIONS

1. Place the gelatin sheets in a small bowl. Add 1 cup of ice, and then water until the sheets are submerged. Let the mixture rest.

2. Combine the heavy cream, milk, sugar, honey, and beets in a saucepan and bring to a simmer. Cook for 15 minutes and then remove the pan from heat.

3. Remove the bloomed gelatin from the ice water. Squeeze to remove as much water from the sheets as possible, add them to the warm mixture, and whisk until they have completely dissolved.

4. Transfer the mixture to a blender, add the goat cheese, and puree until emulsified, about 45 seconds.

5. Strain the mixture into a bowl through a fine-mesh sieve and divide it between four 8 oz. ramekins, leaving about ½ inch of space at the top. Carefully transfer the ramekins to the refrigerator and chill until the panna cottas are fully set, about 4 hours, before enjoying.

Sweet Potato Pie

Yield: 1 Pie

Active Time: 20 Minutes

Total Time: 4 Hours and 30 Minutes

INGREDIENTS

15 oz. sweet potato puree

2 eggs

½ cup heavy cream

1 cup dark brown sugar

1 teaspoon cinnamon

½ teaspoon freshly grated nutmeg

¼ teaspoon ground ginger

½ teaspoon pure vanilla extract

¼ teaspoon kosher salt

1 Perfect Piecrust (see page 217)

DIRECTIONS

1. Preheat the oven to 350°F. Place the sweet potato puree, eggs, heavy cream, brown sugar, cinnamon, nutmeg, ginger, vanilla extract, and salt in a mixing bowl and whisk until smooth.

2. Pour the filling into the crust, place the pie in the oven, and bake until the filling is just set, about 30 minutes.

3. Remove from the oven, place the pie on a cooling rack, and let it sit for 30 minutes.

4. Place the pie in the refrigerator and chill for 3 hours before enjoying.

Squash Whoopie Pies with Ginger Cream

Yield: 12 Whoopie Pies
Active Time: 20 Minutes
Total Time: 1 Hour

INGREDIENTS

6.3 oz. all-purpose flour

1 teaspoon cinnamon

1 teaspoon ground ginger

¼ teaspoon ground cloves

½ teaspoon freshly grated nutmeg

½ teaspoon baking soda

½ teaspoon baking powder

1 teaspoon fine sea salt

7 oz. light brown sugar

2 tablespoons maple syrup

1 cup pureed butternut or acorn squash

1 egg

1 cup extra-virgin olive oil

5.3 oz. confectioners' sugar

2 oz. unsalted butter

8 oz. cream cheese, softened

1-inch piece of fresh ginger, peeled and grated

½ teaspoon pure vanilla extract

DIRECTIONS

1. Preheat the oven to 350°F and line two baking sheets with parchment paper. Sift the flour, cinnamon, ground ginger, cloves, nutmeg, baking soda, baking powder, and salt into a mixing bowl.

2. Place the brown sugar, maple syrup, pureed squash, egg, and olive oil in a separate mixing bowl and stir until combined. Sift the dry mixture into the squash mixture and stir until it has been incorporated.

3. Use an ice cream scoop to place dollops of the batter onto the baking sheets. Make sure to leave plenty of space between the scoops. Place the sheets in the oven and bake until golden brown, about 10 to 15 minutes. Remove and let the cakes cool.

4. While the squash cakes are cooling, place the remaining ingredients in a bowl and beat with a handheld mixer until the mixture is thoroughly combined and fluffy.

5. When the cakes have cooled completely, spread the filling on half of the cakes. Use the other cakes to assemble the whoopie pies and enjoy.

Yield: 1 Tart

Active Time: 30 Minutes

Total Time: 2 Hours

Tarte Tatin

INGREDIENTS

6 to 8 Braeburn or Honeycrisp apples, peeled, cored, and quartered

6.3 oz. all-purpose flour, plus more as needed

1 oz. confectioners' sugar

½ teaspoon fine sea salt

4 oz. unsalted butter, chilled

1 egg, beaten

3 oz. salted butter, softened

⅔ cup sugar

DIRECTIONS

1. Place the apples in a mixing bowl and let them sit in the refrigerator for 24 to 48 hours to dry out slightly.

2. Whisk together the flour, confectioners' sugar, and salt in a large bowl. Add half of the butter and use your fingers or a pastry blender to work the mixture until it is a collection of coarse clumps. Add the egg and work the mixture until the dough just holds together. Shape it into a ball, cover it with plastic wrap, flatten into a 4-inch disk, and refrigerate for 1 hour. If preparing ahead of time, the dough will keep in the refrigerator overnight.

3. Preheat the oven to 375°F. Coat a 10-inch cast-iron skillet with the butter. When the butter is melted, remove the skillet from heat and sprinkle the sugar evenly over the butter. Place the apple slices in the pan in a circular pattern, starting at the center of the pan and working out to the edge. The pieces should overlap and face the same direction.

4. Place the dough on a flour-dusted work surface and roll it out to ⅛ inch thick. Use the roller to carefully roll up the dough. Place it over the apples and tuck it in around the edges.

5. Place the skillet over low heat and gradually raise it until the juices in the pan are a deep amber color, about 7 minutes.

6. Place the skillet in the oven and bake until the crust is golden brown and firm, 35 to 40 minutes.

7. Remove the tart from the oven, allow to cool for about 5 minutes, and then run a knife around the edges to loosen the tart. Using oven mitts, carefully invert the tart onto a large plate. Place any apples that are stuck to the skillet back on the tart and enjoy.

Roasted Strawberry Handpies

Yield: 8 Handpies
Active Time: 40 Minutes
Total Time: 2 Hours

INGREDIENTS

3 quarts of fresh strawberries, hulled and halved

1 cup sugar

2 teaspoons fresh lemon juice

1 tablespoon cornstarch

½ tablespoon water

1 ball of Perfect Piecrust dough (see page 217)

2 eggs, beaten

1½ cups sifted confectioners' sugar

3 tablespoons whole milk

1 teaspoon cinnamon

DIRECTIONS

1. Preheat the oven to 400°F. Place the strawberries on a baking sheet, place it in the oven, and roast until they start to darken and release their juice, about 20 to 30 minutes. If you prefer, you can bake them for up to an hour. Cooking the strawberries for longer will caramelize the sugars and lend them an even richer flavor.

2. Remove the strawberries from the oven and place them in a saucepan with the sugar and lemon juice. Bring to a simmer over medium heat and cook for 20 minutes, until the mixture has thickened slightly.

3. Place the cornstarch and water in a small cup and stir until there are no lumps in the mixture. Add to the saucepan and stir until the mixture is syrupy. Remove the pan from heat.

4. Divide the ball of piecrust dough into two pieces, roll them out into squares that are about ⅛ inch thick, and then cut each square into quarters. Spoon some of the strawberry mixture into the center of each quarter.

5. Take a bottom corner of each pie and fold to the opposite top corner. Press down to ensure that none of the mixture leaks out and then use a fork to seal the edge. Place the pies on a baking sheet and brush them with the beaten egg. Place in the oven and bake until golden brown, about 20 to 30 minutes.

6. While the pies are cooking, place the confectioners' sugar, milk, and cinnamon in a bowl and stir until well combined.

7. Remove the pies from the oven, brush them with the sugar-and-cinnamon glaze, and allow to cool before serving.

Plum Galette

INGREDIENTS

1 ball of Perfect Piecrust dough (see page 217)

All-purpose flour, as needed

5 pitted and sliced plums

½ cup sugar, plus 1 tablespoon

Juice of ½ lemon

3 tablespoons cornstarch

Pinch of fine sea salt

2 tablespoons blackberry jam

1 egg, beaten

DIRECTIONS

1. Preheat the oven to 400°F. Place the ball of dough on a flour-dusted work surface, roll it out to 9 inches, and place it on a parchment-lined baking sheet.

2. Place the plums, the ½ cup of sugar, lemon juice, cornstarch, and salt in a mixing bowl and stir until the plums are evenly coated.

3. Spread the jam over the crust, making sure to leave a 1½-inch border. Distribute the plum mixture on top of the jam and fold the crust over it. Brush the folded-over crust with the beaten egg and sprinkle it with the remaining sugar.

4. Put the galette in the oven and bake until the crust is golden brown and the filling is bubbly, about 35 to 40 minutes. Remove from the oven and allow to cool before serving.

Lemon Posset

INGREDIENTS

2 cups heavy cream

²/₃ cup sugar

1 tablespoon lemon zest

6 tablespoons fresh lemon juice

2 cups whipped cream

Fresh blueberries, for topping

DIRECTIONS

1. Place the heavy cream, sugar, and lemon zest in a saucepan and bring the mixture to a simmer over medium heat, stirring constantly. Cook until the sugar has dissolved and the mixture has reduced slightly, about 10 minutes.

2. Remove the saucepan from heat and stir in the lemon juice. Let the mixture stand until a skin forms on the top, about 20 minutes. Strain the mixture through a fine sieve and transfer it to the refrigerator. Chill until set, about 3 hours.

3. About 10 minutes before you are ready to serve the posset, remove the mixture from the refrigerator and let it come to room temperature. Cover the bottom of the serving dishes with whipped cream and then alternate layers of the posset and whipped cream. Top each serving with a generous amount of blueberries and enjoy.

Carrot Cake

INGREDIENTS

2 cups shredded carrots,
plus more for topping

2 cups sugar

1½ cups all-purpose flour

1½ tablespoons baking
soda

1 teaspoon kosher salt

1 tablespoon cinnamon

3 eggs

1¾ cups extra-virgin
olive oil

2 teaspoons pure vanilla
extract

½ cup walnuts, chopped
(optional)

Unsalted butter, as needed

Cream Cheese Frosting
(see sidebar)

DIRECTIONS

1. Preheat the oven to 350°F. Place the carrots and sugar in a mixing
   bowl, stir to combine, and let the mixture sit for 10 minutes.

2. Place the flour, baking soda, salt, and cinnamon in a mixing bowl
   and stir to combine. Place the eggs, olive oil, and vanilla extract in a
   separate mixing bowl and stir to combine. Add the wet mixture to the
   dry mixture and stir until the mixture is a smooth batter. Stir in the
   carrots and the walnuts (if desired).

3. Butter a round 9-inch cake pan. Transfer the batter to the pan and
   place the pan in the oven. Bake until the top of the cake is browned
   and a knife inserted into the center comes out clean, about 40 to 50
   minutes.

4. Remove the cake from the oven, transfer to a wire rack, and let cool
   for 1 hour before applying the frosting. Top each slice with additional
   shredded carrot before serving.

Cream Cheese Frosting

Place an 8-ounce package of cream cheese, 5 tablespoons unsalted butter, 1 tablespoon sour cream, and ½ teaspoon of pure vanilla extract in a food processor and blitz until combined. Scrape down the bowl as needed. Add 1 ¼ cups confectioners' sugar, blitz until the frosting is smooth, and refrigerate until ready to use.

Roasted Parsnip Ice Cream

Yield: 6 Servings
Active Time: 20 Minutes
Total Time: 24 Hours

INGREDIENTS

1½ cups heavy cream

1½ cups whole milk

3 to 4 cups of roasted parsnip trimmings (the stuff you typically throw away)

Pinch of kosher salt

⅔ cup sugar

5 egg yolks

DIRECTIONS

1. Place the cream, milk, roasted parsnip pieces, and salt in a saucepan and cook over medium heat until the mixture starts to bubble. Remove it from heat and let the mixture steep for 30 minutes to 1 hour.

2. Strain the mixture through a fine sieve, while pressing down on the pieces of parsnip to remove as much liquid as possible. Place the liquid in a saucepan and bring to a simmer. Discard the parsnip pieces.

3. Place the sugar and egg yolks in a bowl and whisk until combined.

4. Once the milk is simmering, add a little bit of the milk-and-cream mixture to the egg-and-sugar mixture and whisk constantly. Add the milk-and-cream mixture in small increments until all of it has been incorporated, while taking care not to cook the eggs.

5. Return the mixture to the saucepan and cook over low heat, while stirring, until it is thick enough to coat the back of a wooden spoon. Remove from heat and let cool. When cool, cover and transfer to the refrigerator. Chill overnight.

6. When you are ready to make ice cream, add the mixture to your ice cream maker and churn until the desired consistency has been achieved. Place the churned cream in the freezer for at least 6 hours before serving.

Black Raspberry Ice Cream

Yield: 4 Cups
Active Time: 30 Minutes
Total Time: 24 Hours

INGREDIENTS

2½ cups heavy cream

1½ cups whole milk

1 cup sugar

Salt, to taste

6 large egg yolks

1 teaspoon pure vanilla extract

5 cups black raspberries

DIRECTIONS

1. Place the cream, milk, sugar and salt in a saucepan, warm over medium heat until it starts to bubble, and remove from heat. Take care not to let the mixture come to a boil.

2. Place the egg yolks in a heatproof mixing bowl and whisk to combine. While whisking constantly, add one-third of the warm milk mixture to the egg yolks. When incorporated, whisk the tempered egg yolks into the saucepan.

3. Cook over medium-low heat, while stirring constantly, until the mixture is thick enough to coat the back of a wooden spoon, about 5 minutes. Take care not to let the mixture come to a boil. Strain through a fine mesh sieve and stir in the vanilla. Set the mixture aside.

4. Place the raspberries in a blender and puree until smooth. Strain through a fine sieve to remove the seeds and then stir the puree into the custard. Cover and place in the refrigerator to chill overnight.

5. Pour the mixture in an ice cream maker and churn until the desired consistency is achieved. Place in the freezer for 6 hours before serving.

Strawberry Rhubarb Ricotta Cakes with Lemon Meringue

Yield: 4 Servings
Active Time: 30 Minutes
Total Time: 1 Hour and 15 Minutes

INGREDIENTS

For the Cakes

4 oz. unsalted butter, at room temperature

½ cup sugar

2 eggs

¼ teaspoon pure vanilla extract

Zest of 1 lemon

¾ cup ricotta cheese

¾ cup all-purpose flour

1 teaspoon baking powder

½ teaspoon kosher salt

½ cup minced strawberries, plus more for garnish

½ cup rhubarb jam

For the Lemon Meringue

1 cup sugar

½ cup water

4 egg whites

1 tablespoon fresh lemon juice

DIRECTIONS

1. Preheat the oven to 350°F and grease a 9 x 5-inch loaf pan. To begin preparations for the cakes, place the butter and sugar in the mixing bowl of a stand mixer fitted with the paddle attachment and beat on high until the mixture is smooth and a pale yellow. Reduce speed to medium, add the eggs one at a time, and beat until incorporated. Add the vanilla, lemon zest, and ricotta and beat until the mixture is smooth.

2. Place the flour, baking powder, and salt in a mixing bowl and whisk to combine. Reduce the mixer's speed to low, add the dry mixture to the wet mixture, and beat until incorporated. Scrape down the mixing bowl as needed.

3. Add the strawberries and fold to incorporate. Place the batter in the loaf pan, place it in the oven, and bake until a toothpick inserted into the cake's center comes out clean, about 35 minutes. Remove from the oven and let cool to room temperature in the pan.

4. To begin preparations for the meringue, place the sugar and water in a saucepan and cook on high until the mixture is 240°F. While the simple syrup is heating up, place the egg whites and lemon juice in the mixing bowl of the stand mixer fitted with the whisk attachment. Beat at medium speed until soft peaks form, about 2 to 3 minutes.

5. When the simple syrup reaches 240°F, slowly add it to the beaten egg whites with the mixer running. Raise the speed to high and beat until stiff peaks form. To test whether the meringue is ready, remove the whisk attachment and turn it so that the whisk is facing up. The meringue should hold its shape. If desired, transfer the meringue to a pastry bag fitted with a piping tip.

6. Remove the cooled cake from the pan and cut it into 8 equal pieces. Spread some of the Rhubarb Jam over four of the pieces. Cover the jam with some of the meringue and then place the unadorned pieces of cake on top. Spread more meringue on top and toast with a pastry torch until golden brown. Garnish with additional strawberries and serve.

Lemon Gelato

INGREDIENTS

2 cups whole milk

Zest of ½ lemon

5 large egg yolks

½ cup sugar

DIRECTIONS

1. In a small saucepan, combine the milk and lemon zest and warm over medium-low heat until the mixture starts to steam. Remove the pan from heat, cover it, and let the mixture steep for about 20 minutes.

2. Add a few inches of ice water to a large bowl. In a mixing bowl, whisk together the egg yolks and sugar. Strain the infused milk into a pitcher, then whisk it into the yolk mixture.

3. Pour the mixture into a clean saucepan and place it over medium-low heat. While stirring constantly with a wooden spoon, warm until it forms a custard thick enough to coat back of the spoon, about 10 minutes. Take care not to overheat the mixture; it will curdle.

4. Place the pan in the ice water bath and stir until cool. Transfer to a bowl, cover it, and refrigerate for about 1 hour.

5. Pour the mixture into an ice cream maker and churn until it has the desired consistency, about 15 minutes. Transfer to an airtight container and freeze for 4 hours before serving.

Strawberry Gelato

Yield: 1 Quart
Active Time: 40 Minutes
Total Time: 6 Hours

INGREDIENTS

1 lb. ripe, sweet strawberries, hulled

½ cup sugar

¼ cup water

2 cups whole milk

2 teaspoons fresh lemon juice

Pinch of fine sea salt

DIRECTIONS

1. Place the strawberries, sugar, and water in a medium saucepan and bring the mixture to a simmer. Cook until the strawberries and become very soft, about 15 minutes.

2. Remove from heat and transfer half of the mixture to a blender. Puree until smooth, add half of the milk, and puree to incorporate. Repeat with the remaining strawberry mixture and milk. Transfer the puree to a bowl and chill in the refrigerator for 1 hour.

3. Stir the lemon juice and salt into the gelato base. Pour the mixture into an ice cream maker and churn until it has the desired consistency, about 15 minutes. Transfer to an airtight container and freeze for 4 hours before serving.

Metric Conversions

U.S. Measurement	Approximate Metric Liquid Measurement	Approximate Metric Dry Measurement
1 teaspoon	5 ml	5 g
1 tablespoon or ½ ounce	15 ml	14 g
1 ounce or ⅛ cup	30 ml	29 g
¼ cup or 2 ounces	60 ml	57 g
⅓ cup	80 ml	76 g
½ cup or 4 ounces	120 ml	113 g
⅔ cup	160 ml	151 g
¾ cup or 6 ounces	180 ml	170 g
1 cup or 8 ounces or ½ pint	240 ml	227 g
1½ cups or 12 ounces	350 ml	340 g
2 cups or 1 pint or 16 ounces	475 ml	454 g
3 cups or 1½ pints	700 ml	680 g
4 cups or 2 pints or 1 quart	950 ml	908 g

Index

About Cider Mill Press Book Publishers

Good ideas ripen with time. From seed to harvest, Cider Mill Press brings fine reading, information, and entertainment together between the covers of its creatively crafted books. Our Cider Mill bears fruit twice a year, publishing a new crop of titles each spring and fall.

"Where Good Books Are Ready for Press"

Visit us online at
cidermillpress.com

or write to us at
PO Box 454
12 Spring St.
Kennebunkport, Maine 04046